The Trickster's Path

A Sociopath's Philosophical Self-Discovery

Alcibiades Anon

ISBN-13: 978-1542836791

ISBN-10: 1542836794

DEDICATION

I dedicate this book to those that have survived me, and added to my greatness. I also would like a special dedication to Dr. S. P. who assisted in editing, framing, and making sure I was not too far off the rails for flies to understand.

CONTENTS

Section 1.

Please Explain

Chapter One

What is This Book?

"Moreover I have felt the serpent's sting, and he who has suffered, as they say, is willing to tell his fellow-sufferers only, as they alone will be likely to understand him, and will not be extreme in judging what he has said or done from agony. For I have been bitten by a more than viper's tooth. I have known in my soul, or in my heart, or in some other part, that worst of pangs, more violent in innocent youth than any serpent's tooth, the pang of philosophy, which will make a man say or do anything.".

Alcibiades

Cultures are filled with tricksters; the Coyote, the Raven, Anasazi, Kitsune, Loki, etc. These are self-centered beings that get what they desire through trickery. They often help and often harm those around them in the pursuit of what they want. They often fail. They sometimes succeed. Neither result matters more than that they acted. They can be short sighted, and yet diligent in their quest. Their impact is so great that almost every culture glorifies them. They are recognized as the catalysts of change. We sociopaths are the tricksters of our species. We face truths others fear. We ignore truths others see clearly. Social norms are suggestions for us. We act in foolish ways that sometimes seem wise. I am here to write a book about us, the sociopaths, the tricksters. A book to discuss a philosophy of what we are. The knowledge we will search out will be about ourselves. How we can build frameworks to become functioning catalysts in a world that is not ours but one we can affect.

What is this book exactly? Why am I coming out of the closet to write? What am I trying to do by outlining, if not filling in blanks into, a fully functioning sociopathic philosophy? Why outline a method of perception and interaction with the reality that most of the world fears and hates? But the word "why" is an elusive pain in my ass. When I ask questions about "why," they usually lead to people hating me and friendships ending. I just cannot form the why questions correctly for most people. My Socratic Method is broken. So, I avoid the why unless someone (usually me) is drunk.

But why, why is a highly functioning sociopath writing a book about the philosophy of being, and how to be, a successful sociopath? It is a question I ask myself. Why am I doing this? I fear it is just an obsession I am feeling. A drive much like any other I feel weekly. Like sex with a specific person or ownership of a specific item. But if it is, I do hope I complete the book. I hope, as all people of a sociopath persuasion hope, that my interest will be held until the end. I know who I am writing it for. The elusive you. The others like me, the spiders. The one in twenty-five humans who see the world the way I do. The sociopaths that live hidden away and desire a way to function among the flies. But who it is for does not answer what I am attempting to accomplish. I am currently of the view that I have a reason, and that reason is clear to me. I will attempt to explain it in this chapter.

First, I am not proselytizing. I am not out in search of converts to the great psychopath nation. Sociopaths are. They just are. Like all things different from the majority, the question becomes: are sociopaths born or made? The idea is that if we are made, then we can be made back. We can be assimilated into normal behavior with a few drugs or maybe a camp. I am not here to debate the issue. I can say if we are made, we are made early on. Paul Sorensen in his book suggests that the newest research looks at genes that might be the cause of our state. These genes open the door for nurture to shape us as we are. Sorensen says that the one combining characteristic of us is that we cannot create connections to others and have no real way to relate to anyone outside ourselves. He puts forth the idea that psychopaths are made while sociopaths are born. The result being the same (or similar), it all becomes a secondary question to what I am trying to frame here.

I cannot remember being different from who I am. I have always been this way and there is no changing me from spider into fly. My life is about my own self-interest, and I fail to find any interest in becoming a fly in a world of so many webs. I assume that those who are flies are equally unable and likely undesiring of becoming a spider. I use these two terms spider and fly in memory of many of those that studied us and called us flippantly spiders. The term spider fits, as does the term masked. Spider is one of the oldest and most widespread tricksters known. I conversely use fly as the spider's prey. Though I have also heard the term empaths used by other sociopaths such as M.E. Thomas. I merely prefer my own labeling system as more colorful. My goal is not to convert those reading into becoming more like me. Honestly, I could not care less about the fact that others are not like me.

Second, I am not attempting to convince the flies to like spiders. As spiders, we need to realize that they hate us. Look at their media, novels, books, and common language. Every time there is some grotesque murder or heinous act, they call the perpetrator a psychopath or sociopath. They write stories about sociopaths who just cannot control their ever-enduring need to kill, steal, rape, and plunder. Look to the fictional view they have of us; the great Hannibal Lector of fiction, TV, and film. He represents how they see us: smart, seductive, and violently evil. Look at the leading expert in criminal sociopathy Dr. Hare. He subtitled one book as "The Disturbing World of the Psychopaths Among Us," and his more populist book was titled, "Snakes in Suits." Telling us everything we need to know about how even the so called objective observers see us.

This dislike is not just cultural. The flies have feared us across the globe and throughout history. Ancient Inuit people suggested we be, "pushed into the ocean when nobody is looking." Most cultures would agree with the Inuit's solution. We have made strides here amongst the flies. At least they no longer think we are diseased. Early on Dr. Cleckley, a seminal expert, struggled with the idea that we could be treated when we are not diseased. Even with his huge list of examples for non-functioning versions of us, he knew we are merely different. He recognized the fact that we had functioning members of our group. The flies have finally begun accepting that we are just different. But even in that, the doctors that make that distinction are still calling us evil. As if evil as a term has any real meaning beside different.

Of course, every study they create talks about how much smarter and more attractive we are than them. They regale each other with tales of our amazing qualities, and yet they treat their personification of us as further proof of our "evil." Watching the media of the flies, I see the obviousness of their fear of anything that is better than them. The pretty girl is always a bitch, and the smart guy is always evil. Look at how they treat smart and attractive women if you ever want to see them beyond their lies. The mere horror that someone could be smart and beautiful is a constant struggle in their fiction (and let's be honest, with their gender normative structure women are often villainized due to greatness). They call us dangerous and violent but look at how they treat anything different from them, look at their hate. They formed the crusades and the concentration camps, and yet we are somehow the monsters. I may speak about my need to survive in their world, but I will never be as hypocritical as they are in their everyday lives. So no, I gave up a long time ago on trying to convince anyone that they should like what we are just because every study they have conducted says that we are more likeable than them.

Third, I am not attempting to talk my brothers and sisters out of the shadows. I am publishing this book as Alcibiades for a reason. The reaction to M.E. Thomas coming out of closet is one example. The hatred they have for us is tangible, and it has real world impact on us. I could not care less how many sociopaths end up in jail, because if you do, it is your own damn fault. But if you are willing to take a little advice, let me tell you they hate you. Some of them may claim to love you, but they love who they want you to be. If you are like me, you can see the flies perceive the world different from what it is. If you are like me, you cannot understand it. You can use it, manipulate it, shape it, but why or how they survive seeing things they want and fear, instead of reality, escapes you. They see you that way. You know this, and know that when they claim to like you, they are liking that perception, that image of you they have. It is not you. They would not like you, not the real you. They would fear and hate you. They would assume you are going to lie, cheat, manipulate, and eventually kill them. You may do some of those for expediency. But it is not like sociopaths are some sort of obsessive freaks that must kill people. Ok so we can be obsessive. You are missing the point. The point is they will never like you. Good thing you do not care.

Fourth, I am not attempting to assist in diagnosing us. We are not afflicted. We are not diseased. And honestly the better the flies are at diagnosing us and finding us, the more dangerous it is for me to be what I am and live a happy life. I am alone, I live alone, I am alone. I not only refuse to be diagnosed under my real name, but I refuse to out myself on these sociopath websites. They are good to join and learn about us (M.E. Thomas's site can be fun) but avoid your real name. I agree with Cleckley in that sociopaths have no interest in their own diagnoses. I go one step further to say they should not have an interest in being diagnosed.

I had three sociopaths this year cross my path. They never knew what I was. Granted they were some of my stupider brethren. But even the highest functioning of sociopaths I can fool for my purposes. The one of this three I had a short term sexual relationship with was almost laughable in her attempt to manipulate me. But it was easy to juggle her, while still pretending to be a fly. I have an obvious advantage with my ability to hold back on self-aggrandizement, but that can come later. To stay functioning in this current society means staying under the radar. It means the flies not being able to diagnose us well.

So, no, this is not a way to discover who is a sociopath in your life. I want us to hide. I agree with Dr. Cleckley that the desire to diagnose our "problem" will never manifest from me. I may not care much what happens to my kind, but I do not want to be the last of my kind, nor do I want to end up in prison or some mental ward. The stigma attached to our diagnosis puts us in one or the other. Honestly, when I recently read an article that mentioned that society should not judge pedophiles too harshly because they have no choice, I was aghast. We need to end these people. And then I was irritated. They used the phrase, "it is not like they are sociopaths or something." I was upset to say the least. I do not hurt children. Children are not special but they are special within society, and though social boundaries are only suggested behaviors, I follow this one. The idea that I am worse than some child rapist… It is offensive. How could I ever allow myself to be discovered by a society that hates me more than the guy that is molesting their kids? More dangerous than the very thing that attacks that which they claim is most precious to them. Their values are that the sociopath who might bilk them out of a few bucks is worse than a pederast. Another example of their values. Add to this the flies are vicious in their hatred. If they hate you, you lose everything, even your freedom. I hope to never be discovered, and I am proud to never be seen.

So, if you are one of us, do not allow diagnosis. Do your best to fool their tests and hide from their hate. We are spiders; the shadows are ours. Even the dumbest of us are smarter than them. We see the world as it is, we experience reality in its purest form. There are no clouds and rainbow bull shit in our perception unless there are actual clouds and rainbows. How simple is that! We are better than them. You are better than them. Too many of us are harnessed by this ideal to be more normal, to be a fly. We are surrounded by people that push us to assimilate. But we cannot, should not, must not be assimilated. At least, not beyond the surface. We are the spiders, and reverting to a fly is revolting, should be revolting. We must embrace what we are.

We must embrace our strengths, while focusing our weaknesses. I do not use silly words from the flies like control. Our weaknesses are often strengths when coupled with luck and focus. We are highly impulsive, and this, when focused, can be a benefit in quick thinking. 70% today is better than 100% too late. Impulse can become a great thing. Honestly, yes it fucks us too often. It endangers us, sometimes in uncontrollable ways, especially when coupled with a slightly overly obsessive reaction to what irritates us. But it is pure, it keeps us pure. It forces us into action, and for a manipulative species that would otherwise play nothing but a slow game, it is a driver to greatness. But it needs to be as focused as it can be. Like all that we are, it needs understood. M.E. Thomas claimed in her book that, “we have alternative means of keeping ourselves in line.” And this ability to focus ourselves is paramount to what we are discussing here.

The best example I can think of is lying. Because it is a form of focus we all learn at a young age. It is one that caused a debate between a friend and me. She claimed her boss was obviously a sociopath because he was an obsessive liar and hurt many people. I disagreed with her and claimed that this was not diagnostic. I base this on every sociopath I have met in life. Lies can be expedient. Lies can achieve goals. Lies are fine and useful things. But there is no obsessive need to lie, not for me. If the truth is more expedient, I use it. I am about self-interest, whatever serves it. This might sound odd to those who are not sociopaths. Yes, our lives are mostly fabrications. When you see me in front of you I am not who is in front of you. We are made up versions of ourselves to appeal to the parts we want to appeal to (or offend the parts we want to offend). But day to day lies, not that important. Sometimes I will tell a lie to test someone, or just because I think it is funny they are so gullible. But for the most part any lie I tell is about expedience. I am goal oriented. Whatever gets me there, gets me there. I have no obsessive need to lie. In my experience, when to lie and when not to is one of the first lessons a functioning sociopath learns. And really if you are not functioning, you deserve your fate as much as the flies. My point being that we must learn to embrace and shape what we are, the positive and negative.

All this I guess leads me to what this book, this philosophy, is about. It is about showing sociopaths how to be functioning. It is about fleshing out our methods in this great world of being the best spider we can be. I started it because I was offended by how many of my kind were searching for answers amongst the flies. The lion does not ask the zebra how to be a better lion. We are strong, we are better than them. And I am offended by those of you that bow to the dictates and advice of those below us. You are making me look bad, and if it is not a manipulation you are working, then I hate you, and I will beat you with a wrench.

I took philosophy before law school. After I am done being a lawyer, I would like to teach philosophy someday. I understand that sociopaths have a philosophical view of the world that is unique and important. We have value. Ok, I have value to me. You being functioning has value to me. If you were to spiral down into overtly bad behavior you would cause society to snap back against me. I do not want that. I want to continue to improve my status and state of being. My book is about how you can assist in that, both for you and for me.

Why should you listen to me? Why am I suddenly the expert on the psychopathic philosophy? Easy: I am better at it than you. As stated before I slip past other sociopaths. I manipulate them as easy as I do flies. The greatest amongst us has been caught in my web and made to pay the toll. I am Anon, I am the highest functioning sociopath you will ever meet. I am a master to your childish Padawan. I am the sociopath that you will never know is in the room. When you attempt to manipulate me, you will realize I made you my bitch. And please do not read gender distinctions into my word bitch. I love strong women, I love women that call me out, and shoot straight. I love the challenge of all strong people, gender regardless. Unlike the flies, when I use the word bitch, I do not mean a strong smart woman. I mean weakness that whines about their weakness. And you will whine, if you are smart enough to even realize I used you, which I suppose is unlikely. I sound like a braggart, but I assure you I am not. In life, I am humble, unassuming, and in control. I am here to help you learn control. To reach new heights of greatness. I want to help you become dominant in your own life.

My hope is that you find value in this book, and you become a better functioning spider because of it. Maybe my book is an attempted manipulation on a grand scale. I suppose if you are a sociopath, it only matters the use you get out of it. The rest of the world can suffer or benefit with you. If you can find use in a systematic break down of sociopathic traits, and the philosophical underpinning that makes it useful in our world, then this book is for you.

Chapter Two

What is a Sociopath?

"I am," is a response, but not the response you are looking for. I have never let anyone know me, so it is an uninformative answer. Psychopathy/sociopathy/antisocial personality disorder is a catch all term for what we are. There are many terms. And there are admittedly in some current systems distinctions between each grouping. But at the end of the day, it is a gradient if distinctions even exist. I believe they might, but the debate is arbitrary and unnecessary for what we are doing here. I do not need to explain all the species of spider to teach you how to spin a web my friend. So, I will go over the basic definition of what we are from my experience as one and from my extensive research.

First, let's look at terms. Antisocial personality disorder, sociopathy, and psychopathy are the important ones. There are those that believe there are distinctions, and those like Dr. Cleckley (oldie but goodie) that believe they are not important distinctions. I tend to think of gradients. Those gradients for this book are not as important as is you becoming functional wherever on the spectrum you fall. Whichever doctor is correct is unimportant and nonsensical for this exercise. We are all spiders. The type of spider is not relevant to this balcony view of how to act and the philosophy of our actions. But what are we? What do we all share? Let's look at the experts, and what they have said.

Dr. Hervey Cleckley created a list in his book "Mask of Sanity." Cleckley reached his prime in the 1960s but is still an expert guide in what we are for the fly community. His book is a great resource on learning more about us. His list of "diagnosing" us is very subjective but still useful.

1. *Superficial charm and good intelligence*
2. *Absence of delusions and other signs of irrational thinking*
3. *Absence of nervousness or psychoneurotic manifestations*
4. *Unreliability*
5. *Untruthfulness and insincerity*
6. *Lack of remorse and shame*
7. *Inadequately motivated antisocial behavior*
8. *Poor judgment and failure to learn by experience*
9. *Pathologic egocentricity and incapacity for love*
10. *General poverty in major affective reactions*
11. *Specific loss of insight*
12. *Unresponsiveness in general interpersonal*

relations

13. *Fantastic and uninviting behavior with drink and sometimes without*
14. *Suicide threats rarely carried out*
15. *Sex life impersonal, trivial, and poorly integrated*
16. *Failure to follow any life plan*

To be honest, Cleckley never numbered his list in "Mask of Sanity." I have numbered it here because it expedites conversation about the items further in the book. I can if needed refer to a specific number easily.

Breaking the list down we find a person who sees the world from a hyper rational point of view. They face no delusions about what the world is, but instead see a clear picture. More clear than the flies. This person has no illusions. They are lacking in basic emotions that plague other humans. In lacking them they react "inadequately" when faced with emotions (unless they have learned to mimic). They do not connect with other humans on an emotional level. They often do not perceive or interact with their world the same way the flies do which causes several disjointed attempts at socialization. Sociopaths for Cleckley are, "a biologic organism outwardly intact, showing excellent peripheral function, but centrally deficient or disabled." Cleckley's examples are big on poor socialization and impulse control.

For Cleckley sociopaths are impulsive, acting out in ways that flies never would unless drunk. They are pushed by obsessive behavior to try no matter what for what they want right now. This can be in detriment at times to long term goals and social norms. But this freedom in their behavior and single minded passion for a desired outcome is attractive to other humans, especially when coupled with a learned mimicking behavior. Sociopaths are missing a morality based on empathy and fear. They are missing internal restraints to stop them from lying or harming others. Thus, allowing for a goal oriented approach to life, that comes across to Cleckley as "pathologically egocentric."

To Cleckley, we have a distinction between our inner world and outer that causes all these damaging behaviors that he sees. We are the perfect mimics, pretending to be flies while internally a source of chaos. Churning just under the surface. Waves crashing in the serenity of our ocean. We are hiding leviathans in our depths. We live a life confused by others feelings while trying to fit in. The boxes and labels of those around us are too tight, too much. We need the boxes to end. We want to be out in the world, and so we try to fit ourselves in the boxes for a time. We can never get everything in the box, and so they see, society sees. We breach the box. We free ourselves without being free. What Cleckley calls a drive to self-destructive behavior, we see as the need to be free of society's boxes, even for just a minute.

Obviously, this list and the words used are judgmental and present the point of view that even when functioning, we are dangerous to society. Labels like "poor judgement" communicate necessarily value, and "ought" viewpoints that are taken for granted and not questioned. As we will see, most experts come from this a priori ideal that how things exist for the majority is how they should be. Other views are potentially dangerous. They see the sociopaths and witness the successes many of us obtain, without ever changing that view. Instead, they grasp at the idea that it is against their slave morality and hence wrong. That said, Cleckley's book is a must read for those of us that wish to better understand who we are, and how the flies perceive us. He is a product of his society. A product of purely clinical experience with us.

The genius of Dr. Cleckley was followed by Dr. Hare who mainly only looked at the criminal element among us. Even having done that, he is the current expert on what we are. He created the test (the checklist) that will be used to diagnose you. It is debatable whether this is so because he is just that good, or because the current society only wants to hear about those of us that live destructive lives. Thus, allowing them to better frame their prejudiced view. For example, his book "Snakes in Suits" is really an excuse for people to judge their bosses as sociopaths.

Hare's 20-point checklist is used mainly to diagnose those spiders already in the criminal system and is often used to keep them there. It bothers me that for no other reason than people being like me, they are held in prisons and asylums. But in the end, they got caught, and so they deserve their fate. They knew or should have known the prejudice existed. He is their main line of defense in finding us.

Hare is quite informative, and a must read if you want to know more about yourself, and the weaknesses of other sociopaths. Hare created the modern-day checklist most often used to find us in our hidden worlds, and it includes looking for a person who is/has:

1. *Glib and superficial*
2. *Egocentric and Grandiose*
3. *Lack of remorse or guilt*
4. *Lack of Empathy*
5. *Deceitful and manipulative*
6. *Shallow emotions*
7. *Impulsive*

8. Poor behavior controls

9. Need for excitement

10. Lack of responsibility

11. Early behavior problems

12. Adult antisocial behavior

As you can see, Hare is much more concerned with our criminal element. But his checklist does include some more objective ideas than Cleckley's and if we are to be honest, it is much easier to read and discuss. The person here, again, lacks emotional connections to others, the past, and the future. This leads them to seem uncaring and to let go of what has already been done by and to them. It frees them to act in ways that those who only think of the future and the past never could. They are free, untroubled, and totally able to achieve immediate goals in ways that are attractive to other humans. It is though in constant tension with the fact that this freedom seems destructive and negative to the flies.

Hare mainly studied us through prisons. He would shock prisoners over and over. He would test them before the shocks where administered to test who felt scared before each shock. If they felt fear they were normal people. Those that felt nothing were sociopaths and ready for further testing.

A few of Hare's items seem highly judgmental. Saying we

exert early and adult behavioral issues seems to forget and forgo all of us that are functioning. Yes, we often act outside of the societal rules and norms, but is it a problem? Do the flies never lie or manipulate? It seems wrong to judge us based on the idea that we do not struggle with our manipulations or feel remorse about breaching social norms. Philosophers throughout time have railed against social norms, and for arguably good reason. Social norms are responsible for such things as slavery and discrimination. Even war on grand scales are usually caused by two groups that just cannot mesh their cultures. I would violate social norms pre-civil rights; I see no reason to not violate social norms now. But the status quo seems to be the strongest driver for the flies. Go to any grouping of flies and suggest a change in procedure. The response you will get first, "this is how we do it."

But enough about that. Let us go back to us. Going over Dr. Cleckley, he seems a bit more vibrant and understanding than Dr. Hare. He seems more clinical if subjective. To Hare's credit, he wrote his books mainly with an eye on sales and aggrandizing his own place in diagnosing us, and at that he is the expert. I can accept and even appreciate that. As such, Hare is a much easier read as it is designed for lay people. Cleckley gets technical, and let's face it, dated. I like them both. Of course, my favorite thing written about us is also by Cleckley in the form of a poem that appeared in the introduction of his book:

> *From chaos shaped, the Bios grows. In bone and viscus broods the Id. And who can say Whence Eros comes? Or chart his troubled way? Nor bearded sage, nor science, yet has shown How truth or love, when met, is straightly known; Some phrases singing in our dust today Have taunted logic through man's Odyssey: Yet, strangely, man sometimes will find his own. And even man has felt the arcane flow Whence brims unchanged the very Attic wine, Where lives that mute and death-eclipsing glow That held the Lacedaemonian battle line: And this, I think, may make what man is choose The doom of joy he knows he can but lose.*

There are other modern experts. For example, Paul Sorensen wrote a short yet informative book where he goes over myths about sociopaths, attributes of sociopaths, and finally a little "how to spot us" section. Though he removes several myths about us, he seems to very much agree with the above experts that we have the potential to be dangerous and destructive.

He does make the point though that we are not evil. Heck, he claims we are not even malicious! Instead he says the truth about us that we just do not care. In the end, we are disconnected from it all, and for us this disconnect feels like freedom. I learned from Sorensen that from the outside disconnection looks like maliciousness. It is interesting that to most people the fact that I do not care looks like I am trying to hurt them. Let's be honest. You might get hurt. You might get helped. Who cares? Me not helping you is not an attempt to hurt you. It is just an attempt to avoid your silly entanglements. The needy narcissism and codependence of the flies is maddening. The four myths he claims are wrongly attributed to us are that we are violent, in prison, psychotic, and all men. He goes over why these myths are prevalent and why they are wrong.

I like that he attempted to remove some myths about us. I also enjoyed his book as it is well written. He also made two extremely important points I think anyone trying understand us needs to understand. 1. "*While their actions may well disturb us, they are perfectly rational to the sociopath.*" 2. "*It's not that they are repressing feelings, they simply lack the capacity in their brain to feel them at all.*" Both statements and many others he makes are quite honest about us. He is honest both in our abilities and inabilities. I can say that everything I have ever done was rational to me, and that every time I have attempted to feel something I found no method in which to do it.

Sorensen then creates his own checklist of our attributes which are:

1. Sociopaths are charming.

2. Sociopaths are spontaneous.

3. Sociopaths feel no guilt or remorse.

4. Sociopaths lie – often and big ones.

5. Sociopaths only love themselves.

6. Sociopaths must win at all costs.

7. Sociopaths are often highly intelligent.

8. Sociopaths are master wordsmiths.

9. Sociopaths will never apologize.

10. Sociopaths are masters of control.

As you can see his list is similar and yet different from the two doctors. His are much more in line with a subjective methodology and I can attest that it would be hard to fully diagnose anyone based on them. But this is not Sorensen's goal. His goal is to help the everyday reader flip through his book and find out if their loved ones are sociopaths. To that end, he makes up for the highly subjective nature of his diagnostic list with a second list. This second list is geared toward warning signs. You simply flip through them, read the descriptors, and decide if those around you need watched closer. Kind of a McCarthyism "is your neighbor a communist" idea. He does suggest not ostracizing these people though - which is nice - just avoiding them when possible. His warning signs list is:

1. They try to manipulate you.

2. *They are top dog*
3. *No empathy.*
4. *Never apologizing about anything, ever.*
5. *Always calm and collected.*
6. *Acts without thinking or regrets.*
7. *You never meet their friends.*
8. *Charming only when it suits them.*
9. *If it feels good, do it.*
10. *Couldn't give a crap what people think.*
11. *Everything is very intense.*

As you can see he is keying in on negative aspects of our behavior. He also indulges in oversimplification in a few areas. I mean, I apologize when it suits me. Like any good lie, it is expedient. I will not attempt to explain the entire list. I mean the book is like eighty pages, and a very good read. I suggest checking it out. He makes some very decent leaps, and is one of the fairest examples of explaining us. His system is simplified for the lay reader to the point of just giving an overview of what to look for. But then that is his goal, and a goal he succeeds at.

Other experts include Martha Stout, who believe being a sociopath is about not having a conscience. For her this is the cornerstone of what we are, we do not have a conscience. We cannot understand the flies because we just lack this one important part. Other groups in the modern word look at more physical ideas such as our ventromedial prefrontal cortex and other parts of the brain being disconnected. We lack this physical connection flies have. We are born different physically. The studies of the experts continue, and grow each day.

But why only look at the definitions of the experts? M.E. Thomas wrote this great book about her life experiences called "Confessions of a Sociopath." This book is both enjoyable and so much better to read than the experts above. She also has a great website I suggest you visit. Her distinction between feeling your body's reaction and the lack of emotional response to that reaction is the clearest view of what we are I have read in a while. It saddens me that so many of us are indoctrinated with this idea that we should feel remorse or guilt, or emotional panic. And yet we do not and we cannot.

Her writing is filled with honest nuggets that scream out at you as you read. We have all struggled as children to learn to mimic. Her statement "I also struggle to react appropriately to other people's confusing and emotion-driven social cues" is genius. Every one of us that is functioning has struggled to hide our internal turmoil. As Cleckley highlighted, we have masks that we impose on ourselves to fit into the world of the flies. Let's face it, that mask is never perfect. As I said before, it is easy to mimic and manipulate. To truly understand emotion is beyond us. The pain they feel, the love, the remorse, the fear. These are beyond us. We struggle to fully understand why we are pretending to react the way we must. We are trapped in a world that is alien to us. If we do not learn from a young age to mimic the aliens, we end up spending our lives in some sort of incarceration. We have the choice of living under doctors and wardens, or hiding our very inner being. Like Mrs. Thomas implies, it is better to "hide in plain sight" than be viewed as we really are.

I have wondered before, what it would be like, to just be me. To be in a world where I could just do something besides hide. I am different; what if I could embrace those differences instead of hiding them. It is a weird statement. There is no me to hide, and yet, hide I do. I know my rambling can get confusing. I can only assume you will either understand or ignore the worst of it.

My own break down on us, my own checklist, is the cornerstone of this book. It will make up the chapters in section two and the arguments for how we are designed to act, and how that design is better and purer than the flies. I will also use those items to create the framework and ethical code (The Doctrine of Experience) that I rely on and go over in section three. So, let's get into my ideas.

I define us in two ways. A distinct list of categories that covers what the experts say, and what other sociopaths think about us. This list is a more objective reasoning about what makes us, well, us. I follow or append this with subjective feelings and thoughts about what we are that go beyond such simplified lists and allows each of us to be unique. This book will break into chapters. Each of the chapters covers one of the objective attributes that I find within us. It will discuss what they are as the drivers of our being. I will include in this how we can focus these attributes to become highly functioning members of society leading to our own success. I will, after this, look at the philosophical underpinnings and the results of the worldview different from the normal human. This will include ideas on our own version of morality as well as the framework we have built in and require to truly be successful in functioning.

I will here and throughout weave my more subjective views that interconnect every attribute we share with each other. I will discuss ways in which each area can be a strength as well as a weakness. I will discuss how to focus our attributes to become our highest functioning selves. I will also interweave several views of the experts, other sociopaths, and philosophers to help elucidate what I am saying. This will require I use several of their views in multiple areas, but as the Buddha believed, everything is codependent co-origination. I will attempt to keep silly repetition at bay even as different areas overlap. My goal here is to help teach you how to becoming functioning in more refined ways.

My check list for sociopathy is rather simple. I use "I am" statements for each chapter:

1. A Mimic
2. Manipulative (Manipulate Rules vs. People)
3. Disconnected (From the Self and Others)
4. Hyper Rational
5. Self-Centric
6. Driven by a Need to Act (Impulsive)
7. Uniquely Focused (Obsessive)

As you can see this list is not in an order of importance but merely in the order in which I wish to discuss them. It is further labeled in a way that I see fit, and not in the normal prejudicial method used by the flies. The list is further not a list of necessary attributes for one born a sociopath. It is instead a list of things we often share. In these we must excel to become functional. I believe that we are rational enough to control the narrative, which encompasses several areas. But I explore "controlling the narrative under "Manipulative."

I start with a discussion of the attribute Mimicry. A

sociopath is a master of mimicry due to circumstances coupled with the rest of the attributes. Though it is not a necessary attribute in and of itself (many non-functioning sociopaths go to jail or psych wards because they do not do this well). That said, it is an important and necessary skill we will discuss, to ensure that all of us are capable of living within society when required. In this, mimicry will become your greatest skill and the shield that keeps you safe. It is hard for non-sociopaths to understand that there is no actor under our act. Perhaps they just cannot understand this is our greatest strength. We are free from those chains of imagined self that hold others. We can become anyone and anything.

If mimicry is our shield than our sword is manipulation. Manipulation is where I focus on controlling the narrative. To truly be successful at both mimicry and manipulation, controlling the narrative is paramount. I will discuss the driving need to manipulate others, but also the very real ability to manipulate rules. Manipulation is a way to exert dominance and control. It is also a way to focus your mimicking and become successful amongst the flies. Violence is not often a very successful way to dominate. Negative reinforcement is often shown to be unsuccessful. These are seemingly easy and short term solutions. But they have no real substance, no style, no panache to speak of. The true artist's manipulation on the other hand is a search for a way to find a real incentive for people to do as you wish. A way for society to do what you want while loving you for it.

The third section will go over our Disconnection. It is often seen among the flies as our greatest weakness. But honestly, the lack of emotional panic and complete freedom of action is a great strength. I will explore the idea that this allows us to seem glib and superficial to others, and still calm in crises. I have already discussed under Sorensen that it often makes us appear malicious because we just do not care. But this disconnect is both with others and with the self, mostly because the self is non-existent. I can be extremely upset right now, and in five minutes not care. Blows can be exchanged. I can be driven to cause pain and hurt, until the drive just bleeds away. I just do not care. I do not care what I have done to you, or what you have done to me. Spiders are free from weird petty holding on to stuff. We are the wind. Locked down by commitments seems silly, when I am born free. But here we are different from other humans, and I will explore this difference, and its benefits.

The third section, Hyper Rationality, is partially an add on to disconnection. Our disconnection means that we are free from emotional blindness. We do not panic at the attack on the self or our beliefs because we have no connection to them. We are free to let our intellect explore all possible ideas. Our perception refuses to be blinded by petty concerns or rose colored glasses. We see what is there. We have no desire to color it in with our own values. We have no values so important. We are free to see. Many researchers claim we almost universally have a higher IQ. I do not think this is true. I think that our lack of connection just allows leaps that otherwise would not be acceptable. By removing fear and the boxes that trap other humans, we are free to truly brainstorm in ways they cannot. This means we at times make connections and leaps that appear as genius. It is just the beauty of free thought.

We are understandably self-centric. My goals are the only goals I care about. If your goals help mine, I will assist you. If not, I need a reason to help. I care about me, and my happiness. How can I care about any other? I work towards my own needs, and I expect you to do the same. I have a driving urge to dominate. My dominance will ensure your compliance. My egocentrism ensures that I require a method of control over you (otherwise your egocentrism may work against mine). I am the alpha. When your strength and wisdom is greater than mine, I accept your leadership. That is until I can usurp you, until I can be stronger and wiser. I may be the apprentice today, but that is merely a time to train and learn all I can to one day become the master.

We are at heart a constant back and forth between the

slow acting attributes covered above and our need to act. We are impulsive. How can I explain this? How do I explain the fact that I have finished a day planning for frugal saving for a current obsession by finding I purchased $200.00 worth of stuff I have no need of from Amazon? I explain it with my driven impulse to act on things now.

There is a need within us that takes over and acts. We lay plans. We build long and previously unthought-of ladders to new depths. But in the end, we just jump into those depths. We have a perception of the world that in many ways would force us to play a slow game. Sociopaths are in this regard very reserved, very shy. We should be very risk averse. But our disconnection from our self, coupled with this need to act allows us to make great leaps (forward and backward). These leaps will at times distance us from our mask, and break us free from our manipulations. In the end, that feeling of free fall is all that matters. Sometimes the slow game gets boring and you need to just take a gamble. Betting the last of your money on a single win gives certain experiences. An addiction absent control mixed with a control obsessed mindset. Only the hyper rational can appreciate the freedom of completely irrational action.

Lastly, we will look at our unique focus among humans. We are known to be a little obsessive. Like me writing this book, or me wanting a pug. I find an obsession; I focus completely upon that desire. And I accomplish it or I accomplish three days of it and let it go. The sociopath's ability to focus allows for great strides forward. It also has the potential to get us stuck in a project few others would have the time for. If it can hold our interest, we will never let go. Happily, things often lose my interest, and so I get away. This focus has an interesting relationship with our need to act. In one moment one saves us from the other, and in the next, they work together to ensure we move in a very specific immediate direction. Of course, the direction is not always healthy or even the best direction possible. But getting free from a stuck rut is always as joyous as finding a new unbreakable need to solve/understand/accomplish.

I will outline and discuss these attributes and I will combine them in the final section. Where I talk about a sociopathic ethical code and framework which I title "The Doctrine of Experience. All in all, we are going to walk through my mind and help you shape yours to fit society better.

Chapter Three

Who I am and the Art of Focus

"Know well what leads you forward and what holds you back, and choose the path that leads to wisdom." Buddha

Like it or not I am a horrible person. No matter what you think of me as I write this book or the things I have done, remember that I am, for the flies, a horrible person. I do not love or hate. I do not frame my life around Kant's idea that people can never be means but only ends. I find it impossible to even understand the idea of not using people. Other people. Other people are the means. Only I am the end. No matter what else you think while reading this, never forget: the author is a horrible person. You are being led through the mind of someone who is probably going to help you up if you fall in the water, but could not care less if you drown. I give to charity. I volunteer. I take up causes you would consider great. But at the end of the day, the world could burn and I would be just as content (maybe even more). I am a master at making you like me, which is why I start the chapter with this warning. If you decide to like me, then like me for what I am, not for what I portray. Otherwise just learn from me. This chapter is a disjointed look at who I am. So, skip it if you desire. Otherwise enjoy the ride.

I am of mixed racial heritage. For most of my young life the light color of my skin was not a benefit. In the area in which I grew up it relegated me to a lower class then others. I still look white, very white. I could care less about race relations or really any societal relations outside of their effect on myself. I see the unfairness that most minorities endure, but my pale skin protects me now that I have left the area of my upbringing.

My ability to mimic others served me well in this upbringing. But my inability to conform always wreaked havoc on my backside. The punishments were constant and often randomly dispersed to ensure that I was both compliant and strong. I am lucky to come from a culture that keys in on strength and weakness in people instead of a sin based morality. As a sociopath, I cannot understand sin or how it works. As a sociopath, I can understand strength. I can form a personal code from it that works for what I am. I am the strongest. I burn away the weakest.

This upbringing focused me on sports and competition. It focused me on winning games, winning accolades. I was not about the practice but the game. Repeated lay ups were not a thing I could handle. But in constant play, I was the wind. I could dance through the forms and continue for hours at a peak level. I have always found that amid chaos, I can internally stop and externally flow. Where the flies' minds go rampant in chaos, my own centers. I become singular, focused. The world stops just for me. I can key in.

Amidst chaos is the least confused I feel. I am made for it. It's why I boxed. The feeling of power amidst the chaos. It focused me, but I eventually gave up boxing as I could never seem to knock someone out. I hated winning on points. I loved to win but this technical tap a tap felt like t-ball. It felt hallow and unreal as a victory. I had to leave the ring. But the focus training gave me, and can give many of us, is essential to who I am today. Focusing my need to dominate saved me. I feel the same impulsive needs as you do; I even give into them. But I focus those impulses as best as I can. I was lucky to be given the framework to channel what I am.

I was also lucky both as I grew up and as I am now, in that my friends and family see me in person for short bursts and then go through long absences. I tell them it is due to work or school. This intermittent frequency in interaction is a system that works for me. I allow these friendships to go fallow so that new growth will return. I have found that my inability to behave all the time can cause rifts in long term friendships. But any idiosyncrasies during the short bursts are explained away as my eccentricity and my need to blow off steam from working so hard all the time on important cases. Creating this view of working hard for long hours keeps me at arm's length. It allows my friendships to grow. Add to this the fact that as my friends get older and outgrow me, I refresh with younger fare, and I am still the wind.

This works because flies naturally pull a veil over their minds as they get older. They become more set in specific thinking and paths. Even when young, they are never fully free, but at least they make the attempt. The young are more lenient with my deviations. They understand my need for no middle lines. Either I could not care less or I am 100 percent bat shit crazy invested. Of course, my buy in needs a quick step toward action, otherwise I revert back into not caring. I have been lucky to fall into these paths early. Now that I see the way, I can take charge of shaping it.

I know that at times I say things that make it feel like I am constantly in chaos and destruction. That is not the whole picture of who I am. I am, from outside appearances, very stable. Yes, I appear to have a disconnection from others, but mostly this is attributed to being so busy. I am perceived as always working, going to school, and traveling. Friends know they can call me anytime and (in their perception) if I can, I will answer and make time. They know that I am not the friend you go to when you need a hug. They know that I will burn a bank to the ground to steal the money and give it to them. I will give my last dollar so they can eat. But they also know that I am very busy, and may not answer. They know not to rely on my being available. I can flake out, but usually for good reason (wink wink). If I can apply myself to their needs, I will. If not they should not count on me.

I am the phoenix, constantly burning away what I was to find out who I will become. Like the historic Alcibiades before me, I conquer, destroy, and reinvent myself regularly to ensure I fit. Alcibiades is the hero of our day. I may leave some pain in my wake, but no more than any other forest fire clearing the way for new growth. I perform my own potlatch every few years, a potlatch of my life. A cleansing giveaway of all that I am to ensure that I stay strong. A ruining of what was, a ruining of me, that opens the door for the new. By freedom from attachment, I am free to cycle through winter into a new spring. I am free to learn without the chains of preconception.

In school, I studied philosophy. I wanted to understand the frameworks of others because I knew that I was nothing like the other humans, the flies. I knew I had no understanding of their rules or viewpoints. I wanted to learn it all. They have this one freedom I do not have. They have the freedom of believing they are an actor and not an act. I have never had that. I have never been an actor, never been a liar, never been a mask maker. I am only the act, the lie, the facade, the mask. This is ultimately my truth. I look within and see nothing, no emotion, no thoughts, no needs. Just nothingness. I am the surface. There is only the mask, the constant empty mask. But unlike the flies, I am changeable. Not set in my ways. I can go on a romantic date with another man and follow it up with baking cookies with my ultra conservative Christian group without a hint of hypocrisy. I can do this because there is no core to me. Not just the external is malleable. I am fully and completely free to become whatever I need. I have no control over what that might be. Like a chameleon, I can become every color but my own. No rest from acting because there is no actor. Can the empaths reading this understand, I cannot just be me, because there is no me?

To help myself understand others, I am constantly creating constructs of other people. I frame them up in my mind and determine their reactions to specific actions. I have become quite good at this building of constructs to the point that I can frame whole imaginary people in my head. This is not some crazy schizophrenic hearing voices. I merely take an idea of a person, say "gay republican" and create a name and character for that person. I then imbue them with all the characteristics that would make sense to them. I then hear this person react to the world around me. I allow them to run free, until they create a system I can work with. I then fine tune it and make changes. Some stylish changes, some changes for consistency, some that just feel right. They become my character of an empathic personality style. A style I can then predict. Understand I have no judgment on their ideas, the goal is merely to create a mimicry of them I can use. The idea of right or wrong in regards to their thoughts is silly. This all works so that I have not only that person but how that person might react. I build these constructs to help me understand and mimic the flies. I have never fully understood them, but I get closer to being able to fully predict them. At the very least I can predict behavior in ways that my own emotionless state does not allow for. It gives me the power to treat others how I think they might wish to be treated, with a bit more accuracy.

But I still needed to understand that nonexistent "me." Philosophy teaches us to seek knowledge, and after extensive seeking towards others I turned inward. I wondered, what am I? For spiders, this understanding is paramount to functioning. We can mimic well without it. But not taking full control of searching for the knowledge of what we are is a recipe for jail time. We say and do things misrepresenting whatever we are. We too often feel the lie within. The lack of a self makes it difficult to stop and be honest about the surface. We must understand ourselves and not our own self-aggrandizement to find our long-term success. Part of this book is simply my walking myself through this dialogue in hopes of fully understanding my success. In private personal internal dialogue, we must at times find honesty.

So, you will hear me say things like I am emotionless and without love. Take this for fact. But also, take it with a grain of salt. Let me explain a few key points. Are you an audiophile? Do you love music, and sounds? If so, my next analogy will make sense to you. You see I am digital and the rest of the world is vinyl. For those of you who are not audiophiles you see vinyl has an almost endless range. Live sounds can range as high or low in frequency as they desire, and vinyl can capture that. Digital on the other hand is not only limited in types of sounds, but in range. You see a digital recording cannot capture the highest highs or the lowest lows. It is limited.

Now take that limit dial and crank it down to a much more miniscule range. I will never hear the great symphony of love. I will never experience it. I see the experience of others and wonder if they lie about it. I will also never experience the depths of depression or sorrow. Your highs and lows are much farther afield then mine. I will never weep for sorrow or joy. I will never feel real anxiety or hope. I have no experience with such extreme feelings. And honestly, I could not care less about those highs or lows.

I do fill with feeling though, and because my range is limited, I fill faster. If one of the feelings in my limited scope becomes filled it fills fast and powerfully. It is all encompassing. A driving force of power and need. A destruction of peace. A totality of focus and obsession. And then it is all gone just as quickly. Read Kant's idea of the sublime and understand I reach that point and lose it in seconds when the same start to finish could take empaths hours. But for those of you like me you will understand. For those that are not you will not. It is that simple. I will never understand flies, and they will never understand spiders. I will never feel the correct emotions in the correct way for them to be comfortable.

It goes beyond not feeling the right feelings. They can never accept that my reactions are legitimate and so they dislike how I react. The unfairness is disgusting. I spend my life trying to accommodate them, but my inability to share a feeling ostracizes me. This means that I do not only react incorrectly but also, I feel the pressure of other people's emotions. The pressure of people trying to see me feel emotions is like bugs crawling on my skin. I react negatively. I can feel their eyes digging into me in judgment. They need to close them. They feel no need to understand. I make the attempt to understand them. But it is too much work to see me. It is too much work for them to let things go when they cannot see me. I am fine accepting them while not understanding them. I just want the same. To be accepted. To be free. To exist without the pressure to join the group they want me to join. To not be ostracized for being different. There is constant pressure circling around other people that expect me to be a fly. It is a spur in my side. I feel like I have been born with wings, but because they do not fit in the world, they get shoved against my back. I should soar, but instead I am held down by flies.

My feelings aren't real. My reactions aren't real. Nothing I say or do is real. From the perspective of the rest of the world I am chasing windmills with a wooden sword. But I don't care. Those giants are important to me. I do not need some fly to understand. I wish to be free. I wish to slaughter these windmills. Kill these giants. Finally feel what life is like without that the shackle of other people. I wonder what those psychiatrist readers who have claimed that we sociopaths are hyper rational will think of all this.

If I could feel hate, I would hate them. But I cannot, so I am constantly over it. I get irritated, but here I am. The impermanence of now. They judge us so harshly. Which of them could forgive such insults? They are obsessed with blame. As if anyone can blame anything but the past. Their obsession with blame drowns us all. But let us be the wind, let it pass through us.

I found a purpose, I found a reason to write this book and help others and myself. I was living a good life. I needed a few changes. I left my comfortable life and practice on a whim to join a protest movement attacking a big business. I became a member of a movement. Strategy was a big part of my life while there, and designing action plans to halt construction. I spent a long time helping shape some of the splinter groups before being forced away on another adventure. I did not wish to leave, but I had to. I promised to come back.

As I left the group, I knew I had to come back. I felt the pull from the old lady beside me in the night. I knew she was not "really" there, but I felt her, and we understood each other. I understood I could find a purpose if I stayed strong. I was anxious for the first time in my life. I felt a long hollow tube was filling me with uncertainty. I had never experienced this discomfort and it was disturbing and liberating at once. I had found my own personal Bacchanalia and needed only to embrace it. I felt the need to go back, to help, to be a part of this joy. The idea of helping was unimportant, what I loved was the destruction, the ruin of such a huge company that thought it could destroy us all for its own goals. Little did it know my own profits came first. And my profit, the joy of ruin, was here to stay.

I would slam my hammer against the anvil of their billons and I would shape a new world.

These protestors had helped me learn to harness my joy of ruin into a worthwhile goal. I reveled in this use, this glorification of my abilities. I could focus my intelligence. I could rely on my impulsivity. I obsessively zeroed in on a set target to ruin. I reveled in the glory and accolades I received in the group. It was chaos. I was again centered in that moment of chaos. I was even able to convince them that I needed to remain hidden from cameras. Nonprofit protest groups are perfect. This might be my calling. I am convinced it was time to change to this new and beautiful thing. Using all I had learned in strategy and business to help shape a movement of such magnitude framed my being. I could liberate every part of me, and sink my claws into life. I wondered, is this how normal emotional people feel? Is this what is to be free?

The entire experience made me wonder, can I be this way all the time, and if so how. I have been successful when so many of the other spiders are squashed. Again, how? I spend about thirty percent of my life prepping for a certain image I desire to give off. Much of it is never seen or commented on by others. But I know it, I feel it. It is all part of creating me. I live in the now, but to ensure future success in my life "how" is a paramount question. I have always been proactive about shaping and controlling myself in ways to ensure that I excel. I am the best. I am better than normal humans because of my attributes, but I can always be better. I can fit. I can even excel in their world. I have excelled and found excellence wanting. But how can I take better control? This question drives me. And I know that I have spent my history focusing. But now it is time to focus better.

I call what I do focusing. I focus my sociopathic traits to improve their effectiveness. I prepare set responses in the emptiness of myself. I think through possible conversations and interactions to prep for those possibilities. Most wasted, but some not. I have a need to multitask to fully experience the world. This creates moments where I have the time and energy to be ready. I have currently become obsessed with the idea of game theory. To me game theory is currently the best theory to harness and focus my personal needs and attributes. I feel like flies can be desensitized to the emotions of others. It is my theory that we can become sensitized to them. Not that we can fully comprehend what others are going through. We never will feel. But we can become more cognizant to predict reactions. The fly who becomes desensitized will always still feel the pain deep down, we will never feel it. But we can cover that lack just as they can cover the pain. By focusing our needs and creating a system that reinforces us in mimicking behavior we can fully capture the best functioning sociopath we can be.

The art of focus is simple. You create internal reasons to focus toward specific goals and focus away from certain negatives. A quick study of game theory shows us that simple rewards for simple actions should occur immediately. It became recently popular with things like trophies in video games. These trophies keyed in on specific random acts that the game creators wanted to encourage. You killed 10 grunts, you get a trophy. Kill 50 get a better trophy. Some of them are silly and some are difficult. They teach you that to be the best you need more than everyone else. The quest to obtain them becomes as important as finishing the game. Now recognizing that every sociopath is an individual, I allow that you need to create your own system. Forgoing discussion of my control of your choices here, I allow you this freedom from my dominance. This is both easy and difficult. Just ask Dr. Fallon, the doctor who laughingly discovered he was one of us. It is as easy as creating a system of red, gold, and black stars you can reward yourself mentally. One red star for each day you say something nice to someone, a gold for a week straight, and a black for a month. Simple. But how do we get it right?

We know we have started to get it correct when it starts to modify our behavior. A simple way to start modifications is to give a small incentive when you have reached a specific level. I can buy an expensive coffee bean for myself after so many social acts. I create the game. I play the game. I cheat the game. I game the game. But in the end, I play the game. The game helps me to focus on becoming more functional. As I said before, I am the most functional sociopath you will ever met. I am unseen by others, and shape the world around me. I will never do jail time, and I shall never suffer for my difference. If I am discovered, I will laugh and convince you it is a joke. I will reassign values to myself and then my world to ensure my success. I will manipulate my being and through that the beings of everything around me. But the first step is focus. I use game theory to ensure I stay on track.

I have always known that life is a game. You know it, you feel it. I just play it better, so play with me. I am here to help you learn to play it even better. Because the more sociopaths are amazing members of society, the better off I am. The more likely I can stop hiding, is more of my energy that can go to better uses. I can, through this game, focus on competitive and manipulative behavior. I can enjoy success through competing with others and myself. I can manipulate everyone including myself into the best world I can imagine. Imagine with me.

Now I know that some will ask, "when do we win the game?" This question is stupid. It is a symbol to me that you are not a sociopath. You see there will never be a win or lose. I said it before there is no relax and be ourselves. There will be a win, but not a Win. Battles will be fought and conquered but the war will never be over. You see there is a desire to achieve the goal. To reach home port. But no port, once achieved, is as invigorating as the insanity of the open ocean in full storm. The struggle to survive is the price (and joy) of a fully lived life. The impermanence of the game is all we have. Like a good piece of sand art. We live our lives making it fantastic, only to let it wash away. Our victories and defeats are only momentary. The flies may wish to hold on to the now with clenched hands, but never us. We are free of such craving. We play the game to play. Winning or losing are just excuses to start a new game.

Ozymandias

I met a traveller from an antique land
Who said: Two vast and trunkless legs of stone
Stand in the desert. Near them, on the sand,
Half sunk, a shattered visage lies, whose frown,
And wrinkled lip, and sneer of cold command,
Tell that its sculptor well those passions read
Which yet survive, stamped on these lifeless things,
The hand that mocked them and the heart that fed:
And on the pedestal these words appear:
'My name is Ozymandias, king of kings:
Look on my works, ye Mighty, and despair!'
Nothing beside remains. Round the decay
Of that colossal wreck, boundless and bare
The lone and level sands stretch far away.

Percy Shelley

Section 2:

About Us

Chapter Four:

A Mimic

It is funny how we define ourselves. How we see ourselves. It is funny how we define the image that is us. I was home tonight ready to write this chapter. I had told everyone I was going to bed, not to bother me. I was busy. But I did not go to bed. I was alone, drinking. I had spent 10 minutes perfecting the perfect old fashioned. I then enjoyed it while tasting the finest cigar I had at the moment. All this to really feel the mood I wanted to feel.

Even in this time of solitude I was creating an image. I had expensive whiskey and a nice cigar. Not that I like either, but the image of who I am does. And as I had to get up and leave the computer to refill my old fashioned, it hit me. I am alone with a computer and $300.00 worth of drink and smoke. I am alone and drinking this expensive whiskey I do not even know if I like. All because the image of me I want to portray drinks only the best. Do not get me wrong I can bore you with all kinds of whiskey facts and whisky facts. I can bore you with cigar talk and how to make an old fashioned the "right way." But is that me? Do I really care?

I spent months creating my own soaked cherries. So much work growing my own blood oranges on the tree I planted. Finding the perfect muscovado took research and money. All of this, for an image. An image right now only I see. I am hollow inside so why would I care? I mean I am alone here with my computer, and yet the illusion is alive and well. The illusion that is me. I am not addicted to the nicotine in the smoke or the alcohol in the drink. Instead I am addicted to the image of smoking and drinking the way I do them. I may have no connection to other humans but I am addicted to creating an image I want them to see. And this brings us to the first attribute we will discuss and the first skill you will need to perfect.

In this chapter I will go over why we mimic mixed with why we need to. Like all chapters in this section mimicking is an attribute of what we are. These attributes will be split between potential weaknesses you will need to focus into strengths and skills you need to practice to strengthen. Your ability to function rests on your ability to mimic. The strength of staying off the radar and becoming a member of society relies on your success here. This success will be paramount to the next chapter Manipulation.

The current view of sociopaths is that we are charming. If you wish to follow my footsteps, then perfecting this yourself should be a source of pride. It is our legacy. The fact that we have learned that we are antisocial is no reason for you to be asocial. I will discuss how to prefect your skills of mimicking through the techniques I use. This will include creating internal constructs of personality types you fit other people into. It includes finding ways to learn how to study emotional reactions and the correct responses to those reactions. This should be easy once you have the basic ideas to practice. Much of what we do will be interdependent on other attributes, but these areas will be cross referenced.

Let us discuss why we mimic. We mimic for five real reasons. First, because we would be hated by the flies for our differences if we did not. This is tied into the second reason which is that we are disconnected from others and any idea of self. Third, we face a truth few other humans face which is that there is no internal self, only the image we create. And fourth, because we are addicted to that image we created, addicted beyond what makes sense to others. Lastly, and a very important reason is to obtain our goals. To ensure our manipulations are successful. To ensure that we can have those things we enjoy. We mimic for many reasons.

First, if we revealed our lack of self we would be hated. Flies hate things that do not fit into their limited world view. They require the lie of an internal self, the lie that humans care. They require the imaginary pretend world that we are something inside. Flies feel love and hatred for others. They cannot comprehend that we feel nothing back. But we must face the truth, the truth that we are nothing. Like the Buddha before me I face a reality of no core self. But that view does not fit what the flies want. And so, I need to hide. We need to hide the fact that we just do not care, that there is nothing to care about. Remember my words and hold them tight to your chest. Because of our differences we need to hide.

Cleckley discussed that our biggest flaws come out in social settings. The best way he could think of to spot us was in how we react incorrectly in groups. He paid special attention to those reactions that "to a normal man are the most profound." He recognized that we are superficially quite good at being popular in limited circumstances. But in more emotional or long-term situations, we often reveal ourselves. Because of this we need to practice. As a natural state, we grow uncomfortable in emotional situations. M.E. Thomas spoke eloquently about her inability to handle and her discomfort with the highly emotional situations. We are not built for such drama, it is alien to us.

We face the truth that we have no self. Those flies that have embraced rational thinking, like the Buddha, understand that we have no internal core self. Because of this we are free to become whomever we desire. Ties to unnecessary personhood are silly. We have no need for such arbitrary attachments. We are free of all attachments. We can embrace the chaos of the world, because we have no true self to hold us back. You see flies they have these human attachments to the self-such as sexuality, religion, homophobia, philanthropist, or connoisseur. But not us, not the spiders. We are free to embrace whatever image is needed right now. The philosophy of Buddhism (outside and inside the religion) embraces that we are not our consciousness, but our drive.

We are our intent, our will, our drive. In a Buddhist metaphysical sense, we have only five attributes (Skandhas), and they are: 1. Body/Form, 2. Sensations/Feelings, 3. Perceptions, 4. Mental Formations, and 5. Consciousness. The core of Buddhist thought is that we are none of these parts, and yet these parts make us up. Suffering in Theravada Buddhism comes when one clings to one or all the parts as the self. This suffering is caused because we have no self, and attempting to grasp onto something that is not there is just another method of attachment and craving. The Four Noble Truths relegate all attachments as the cause of suffering and each must be let go of before one can be free. The goal then is to realize you are not these parts that make you up; you are nothing. Sociopaths have this truth built in.

The example given in Buddhism is that of the chariot. To modernize let us say the car. Is a car the tire? The engine? The steering wheel? What part of the car is the car? If I slowly replace every part of a car, at what point does it become a new car? Let us say I have two cars. I exchange parts between them. At what point does one car become the other and vice versa? The point of the thought is that we are not our parts, we are not the whole. We are not a being, but a becoming. I will go more in depth on this idea in the chapter on disconnection but for now it is important to understand that you have no self beyond your current intention. Intention is all you have. Anything you represent will not reflect the "real you" because there is no real you.

Spiders are disconnected from the self and others. This disconnection will be covered in its own section because disconnection is one of our key attributes. But it is good for a beginner step here. We mimic because we have no self. We mimic because we are not connected to others. Our only connection is what we create as a false persona. It lasts as long and as deep as we use it. Accepting this needs to happen now, and the nitty gritty of it will come later. Facing our reality is a big step for us. We are trained to think we should be connected to others, that we should be connected to ourselves. We are indoctrinated by the flies. Our youth often face a confusing world that does not fit with what they are constantly feeling. Let us embrace the truth. It does not matter what others are or think we should be. We have no self. We are free of all things because we are hollow. Embrace your freedom. You are only holding onto this image of you because of your addiction to that image. Be free.

We are muddled through our addiction. It holds us much like the fly's belief in themselves as a Self. To embrace true adaptability, we must be capable of breaking free from the addiction when needed. We have a course, but that course is not always correct. And it should never be set in stone. We must face the facts that our gut instincts are at times wrong. Creating the image, we want is not always enough. At times, we must deflect the image others are attempting to hold on to. As M.E. Thomas says it is not always enough to hide what we are, at times we must "poison the well with disinformation." So be mindful not only of the image you are creating, but also the image you are seeking to hide.

There is a war within you in. First, you feel a need to act out (what some call impulse). This fights the unique focus on things that we cannot shake loose (a focus sometimes called obsession). But there is a balance between the two. To be functional we must buy in, even when alone, we buy in to our current persona. But we must also understand that persona can become counterproductive, which means we might need to change. I can put in months learning the best wines, but in the right company, I need to become an expert with craft beer. We must balance our addictive focus with our impulse to act now. Embrace both, and practice how we can improve our mimicking. It is not always enough to know the best wines. We must become the best at all things, to enjoy every company, and fit into any situation. You will have goals and manipulations in the works and your mimicking will help you achieve them. Because of this let us look at how to improve our skill set.

The how's of mimicking are at their base a practice of techniques mixed with art. Put in the time, become better. Or get lazy, and fail. Fail at your manipulations. Fail at your life. Fail at everything you are attempting to accomplish. But if you do not want to fail, then practice. Work, get better. Become an artist.

Remember that the flies tell themselves stories. They lie constantly to themselves and others. The have this fiction in their mind of what they are and their place in the world. They make up parts for everyone else in their world to play. They want villains and heroes, love interests and good friends. They expect others to play the part. The purpose of mimicking is to fit into the role they want you to play. That is the only role that matters to them.

You can see them struggle when others do not fit. They have a script in their minds of how things will go, and it is like they can read nothing else. Their script is hard to edit. This first chapter is fitting into the existing script, after which we will move on to editing the script with manipulation.

The Chinese philosopher Chuang Tzu told a story that highlights this blindness within the flies. He told the story of the Proto-man. Proto-man was here long before other living creatures. He was different from all the others though in that he looked like a human but had none of the standard nine orifices of a human being. The first humans struggled to survive because they knew not how to grow their own food or prepare for winter. But Proto-man knew and he helped them. And due to his teachings, they learned how to survive. The humans gathered together and debated how to repay his kindness. They decided to give him the 9 orifices so he could enjoy them all the ways a normal human enjoyed them. They held him down and started to drill each hole where they belonged. Per Chuang Tzu he was so 'grateful' he died by the third hole. The humans refused to see him as he was. He stood right in front of them, yet they still failed to see he required his differences. They saw only that he was different. We have the benefit of being able to function in society by hiding our differences.

If you want to function you need to create and then practice being a functioning persona. There is no other way. You first study those around you. Then you study their reactions to situations. You build constructs of personality types in your mind to practice how they would react, and hopefully learn to predict real people. You will never experience the world the way they do, but you can hope to react accordingly. Lastly, you will practice your ability to study and build your internal constructs in situations where you can be anonymous and safe. Through these methods, you will slowly improve your methods at mimicking.

First, you need to study. M.E. Thomas suggests observation and pattern recognition. She is correct. You will never be a fly. You will never accept Jesus into your heart and feel what the Christian feels. You will never experience the love of another person and feel the acceptance and warmth they feel. Even hate, that all-encompassing hatred, they feel will never hold you. You are the wind, and your disconnection keeps you free of all that internal rambling. Cleckley brings up our blindness succinctly. "We find ourselves dealing not so much with a genius at acting but with a person who, in the most important matters, has no capacity of distinguishing between what is acting and what is not." We need to overcome this weakness, take charge of it. Because of this you need to study yourself and the flies. Study the patterns. To be a great mimic you must learn to improve your facade. You must watch those around you. What makes them cry. What makes them laugh. You do not need to feel the pain of loss to know when you should look sad. You must watch as many people as you can.

The beauty of today is that we have movies, books, internet, and so many areas to look to see how flies react. How they think we should react. And let us be honest how they think we ought to react is more important than how they themselves would react. There is a very real disconnect from how they tell us we should be and how they are. We need to be able to mimic both, even if we can never understand either. They have a fiction, the fiction of who they want to be. Humans prefer who they want to be then who they really are. This fiction is an important tool. Read as much as you can. Study books, movies, and TV. They have a host of fictional areas you can delve into. And if you want real world experience go people watch. Be nosey, just study. You can read their social media and learn how they think and argue. Learn how they think they ought to behave.

Make lists mental or in writing. Lists of things that happened and how people reacted. Become Google studying big data. Let go of the idea of causality and embrace the idea of correlation. You will never understand. Why look for a cause you are unlikely to see, and less likely to grasp. What you want to look for is correlation. "Y" happens, people react with "X." Learn the Y's and the X's and start to make lists of those correlations. You are surrounded by flies, watch and learn. I know it is tough. Looking at them there is nothing but confusion. Once you let go of trying to make order of that confusion, and embrace the chaos that is, you will open doors you never thought you could.

An importance of this open door is the creation of internal constructs. Let me explain. I create an idea around what I fail to understand. Like Hannibal Lector creating a mind palace I create a town hall of voices that can inform my behavior. For example, my favorite construct is a flamingly gay republican. I do not understand this group's attributes that appear from the outside to be contradictory. To create the construct I start with a name. Nothing I am attached to, just something to start us off. I create the idea of Christian Johnson a gay republican. I fill in all the details of Chris I can. Not like creating a character, but creating a voice. He is flaming, he has certain specific framings of words and colloquialisms that I can predict. The voice in my head I create and I begin to ask it questions. I frame the answers over and over until Chris becomes an actual voice in my head I can talk with. I can ask questions of him. I can give hypothetical situations to him. Any situation I put him in I can hear his response. I go back and forth with him getting answers. I take those answers and compare them to actual gay republicans. Those that fit I keep, those that do not I change. Slowly over time I create the construct of Chris. A person I experience in my mind that reacts to what I am experiencing in his own way.

His experiences may only be my constructs of how he would react. But let us face it, by creating him, I know how I should react if I am in a situation where I need to be or need to deal with a gay republican. Having one or two of these constructs is helpful, but as you build more and more you become more adaptive to situations. I often lay in bed waiting to sleep rolling through examples of different constructs, let the different voices have conversations. I give them hypothetical situations and let them react. If you do this their reactions inform you. I do not need to understand Chris. I only need to understand how he would react. Now I can, if needed, be a gay republican. That is what I need to mimic that group. I want to function. I find a situation where he is the most efficient use of me. I can be him or I can deal with humans like him. I need a homophobic backwoods democrat, I have him as well. This sounds like I am creating multiple personalities. I am not. I am creating internal constructs that I can use to study human behavior. Having no self, I am obviously not any of these people. But researching each stereotype means I have a better method of predicting flies' behavior. I understand all my skills only work if I use them. For that I need a safe place to try them.

So now you have mimicking structures, you need to find ways to practice them. Groups you can be anonymous in are perfect. Go to a bar in a different city, or a class/group among strangers, and you are open to practice. If you fail, and reveal yourself, you just go home. Practice amongst those that do not matter in your life. Find groups that have no connection to your current manipulation group. Ensure you do not risk your social circles to practice. AA meetings, and any anonymous groupings are useful. But nothing beats going out of town. When faced with somewhere new you can create an entire persona to try. It is good to practice. Improv groups are great practice. Because let's face it, you are always on stage, and you never know when you must think on your feet. Go where you can test new personas.

Remember that who you are creating is incomplete. People love a riddle, they distrust when everything is laid out before them. Take your time, do not feel the need to have all the answers. A compulsive liar is easy to spot, because when questioned they will never reach a point of unknowing. You ask about things they have no reason to know anything about, and magically they have an answer. Usually wrong, but still, an answer. This is a weakness that allows them to be spotted. So always recall that you should not have every answer, and just because you do have it does not mean you should share it. Instead as part of your practice at least once a week feign ignorance of a thing you know and want to share. Give someone else a chance to show off, it will make you more appealing to the person you let be the hero.

Which brings us to the last technique of any functional sociopath. You need a break from being a fly. Cleckley recalled a fellow psychiatrist that was a sociopath. This doctor was well respected in his field, and ran his own very successful hospital. The doctor had an amazing success rate with patients, and Cleckley remembers how excited students were to meet him. This man was in many ways the epitome of his field. But he took regular trips out of town, trips that Cleckley discovered were to other towns that considered the doctor a drunk and extremely disagreeable. The doctor used these regular vacations to shake off the respectable shell he wore day in and day out. We all need this. We all need a break from the mask. A place where we can just let go and let chaos take over. These breaks recharge, and revitalize our ability to keep the mask in place.

In conclusion mimicking is vital. It is important to understand why we mimic. We mimic for five real reasons. We accept that we are nothing, and this acceptance would lead to us being hated. We have no real connection which allows us to freely associate as we see fit, both internally and externally. We understand that we are no more than the image we create, a truth few humans are willing to embrace. We are mimics because we are addicted, like a smoker who smokes because it looks cool and not because we enjoy it or are addicted to nicotine. We have real internal images to mimic. We have goals and needs that we want met, and mimicking is part of that manipulation.

The ways in which we mimic are through both internal and external study of the society around us. We look at real world situations coupled with internal constructs that assist us in predicting other people's reactions. We must let go of trying to understand, and embrace trying to predict. In this everyone becomes happier. We practice our new-found observations in safe ways. And we must find moments where we can let go of the personas we have created. Mimicking is a vital skill and an inherent ability to all sociopaths. We must continue learning better and more accurate methods of predicting how flies would behave so we can accurately mimic those actions.

Chapter Five:

Manipulative

As a sociopath, I am on a constant search for power and dominance. I have defined and undefined desires and goals. One powerful tool I have for obtaining those desires and goals is the art of manipulation. We manipulate in three main ways. First, we control the narrative in which we are perceived. We do this through mimicking what is desired and understanding what others want. We are in a sense manipulating the image of ourselves. Second, we manipulate rules of our society and groups. Those rules define the game we are playing and learning to understand them and shape them is an ingredient to success. Third and finally, we manipulate the people within our group. We find ways to study the systems and assign value to the people with in the group. We understand the game then play it until completion. Once done we move on to a new group. We perfect all of this through practice. But first the overarching idea of manipulation is how do we control the narrative and make sure the world is telling our story.

A. Controlling the Narrative:

Sociopaths are known for our ability to manipulate both other people and rules to fit into our agenda. It is believed that we use superficial charm and our heightened intelligence to position people in ways that we want. Most people call what we do deceitful, insincere, and malicious. I call it goal orientated narrative control and/or motivating/incentivizing. We exert our dominance, and show that we are the ends through action. Everyone wants something and as M.E. Thomas expresses we find ways to facilitate exchanges with others to ensure we get what we want. The best result obviously is a win-win. I want my employees to put out more work, and they want better benefits. Both groups are trying to manipulate the other. If I can incentivize their behavior and motivate them through my actions, we both win. That said, if they get what they want then all the better, if not, they should have negotiated better. It is not my job to ensure they succeed in their goals only mine.

To ensure that I control the narrative in ways that benefit me I focus on the goals I wish to achieve. These goals can be simple or they can be complex, but I focus on them. I drive the interactions with others toward that goal. I set up my mimic persona to position me to be ready to take advantage of situations that can be maximized, while preparing to minimize the harmful effects of negative events. My persona both in action and in words highlights what I want highlighted and shadows that which I wish hidden.

How do I accomplish this? I concentrate on controlling the narrative as I have been describing. That is my main goal. I use all my skills together including my mimic persona to control the experience of me that others experience. I then look at two main areas I can manipulate in the world around me. First, I manipulate rules. Oh, the flies love their rules, and finding ways to fit them to my needs is an important step. I follow this up with manipulating the people within the rules to positions I want them to be in. Of course, these two areas require balance. If you are too apparent at manipulating rules in the wrong ways other people get upset and see it as unfair. The world is unfair, but the flies like to believe it is fair. So be wary of letting them see you manipulate the rules in ways they will disapprove of. Instead it is often better to manipulate another person into fitting the rules into your needs for you.

I will go over ideas on manipulating others and ideas on manipulating rules in a moment. Why we manipulate though is an important question. Sociopaths have a driving need for dominance. We seek out power for the sake of power. There is an inner drive to be the best and prove to ourselves that we are the best. From M.E. Thomas' discussion of predators and "Surplus

Killing" we can see that we will be driven to manipulate even when there is no need. In her book, her blog, in expert reports, and in my own life I have experienced the need to "ruin" both others and myself.

Surplus killing is a common activity amongst predators. It is the house cat the kills mice and birds even though they have a full dish. They kill because they are driven to it. They are practicing skills they may one day require. It is a unique and scary part of the predatory world that they will kill and hunt for no other reason than the joy of killing and hunting. For sociopaths, it often comes in the form of manipulation even when no manipulation is required. Externally people see it as a self-sabotage when applied personally and malicious when applied externally. But deep down it is neither.

The results are not as important as the fact that I can cause it to happen. Can I upset someone enough to hit me? Yes, then I win. It does not matter that I get my ass kicked if I lose. It does not matter if I get fired. What matters is that I caused the reaction to happen. I wondered if I could force behavior on someone else, and I did it. I can upset parents into a beating. I can cause a party goer to "go ballistic." I can make someone else feel happy or loved. I can control behavior, and how that reaction affects me is not always as important as the fact that I can cause it.

Similarly, my more impulsive manipulations of the ruin of others lacks any real malicious intent. It merely reflects my wanting to exert my dominance by causing things to happen. When confronted by a man that was attempting to sexually harass young girls M.E. went on the attack. She was driven to ruin him. M.E. explains, "I was never one to be greedy or get caught up in the 'principle of the thing.' I wasn't trying to get him fired to protect future generations of vulnerable young girls. I was trying to get him fired to show him that he was vulnerable, and to me, a helpless little girl." His actions against her did not offend her or cause her real suffering, but they opened the door for him to be ruined. She practiced her manipulation outside of her goals and proved to herself and others her power.

Again, there needs to be a balance here. Spiders are driven to surplus kill, to manipulate and dominate even when it could be destructive to our goals. We must focus this. We need to ensure that when we feel these drives we can express them in ways that are healthy for our bottom line. As a young sociopath, I cannot explain how many times I ruined a long term good thing by an impulsive need to manipulate. Sometimes it worked out for the better, other times not so much. I now prepare for this eventuality in ways that allow me to mitigate the negatives. I start with the assumption most relationships will not last more than two years. I further take time where I can break from character in other towns or safe places to ensure that I can relieve the tension.

Much like the final step in mimicking, it is important that we face the fact that our impulses and obsessions are going to act out eventually. We face that reality. We must find ways to give in while still remaining goal orientated. If you can relieve the tension by getting away and acting in a separate group, then I suggest doing it. If the obsession is geared toward one thing/action, it is tougher. You need to find ways to mitigate backlash. Intermediaries are good here, but better is planning. Take an action that the person being manipulated is unlikely to see as ruin. You are driven to humiliate a boss that is just aching to be taken down a peg. Rather than try to destroy them professionally which could potentially be hugely negative for both you and him/her, why not seduce the boss into a homosexual affair. Most flies avoid sex talk, and homosexual sex even more. You can prove your ability to manipulate them, while remaining off the world's radar. The point is that you controlled the situation, you won. This can be a host of actions taken on your part, and it is important to get creative.

Dominance comes in many forms, learn to embrace each form. The highly violent sociopaths are trapped in the belief that dominance comes through violence or equally destructive behavior. Do not believe this. I once paid for an irritating 'friend's' Christmas for their family. Why? Because I could, because I was better than she was, stronger, dominate. I had the power and by acting she knew it. Her family knew it. Those she told knew it. I never held it over her head, I never mentioned it to anyone. I knew she would, and even if she did not, why would I care. I won through kindness, a lesson all sociopaths need to learn because it is counter intuitive, yet so sweet. I did this because that is what the powerful do, they show mercy to the weak as a subtle exertion of their power. And through my focus I could not only mitigate the damage I might have done by publicly ruining her, I came out looking like a hero. I am a hero.

Like you I struggle with surplus killing. The impulsive drive to act at times to ruin a person for nothing. To exert my dominance right now. But I focus, I focus on the narrative I am trying to create. I use words and actions to highlight what I want others to see and hear. I shadow and hide away those things I do not want them to experience. I ensure that the narrative is so firmly in my control that if someone accuses me today of being a sociopath the response will be, "But he is so nice." And I am actively changing the landscape of my acquaintances that hopefully one day the reaction will be, "I know isn't he so sexy." I know it is a dream, but a dream I am fulfilling.

The philosopher Nietzsche discussed two main methods people use to embrace ethics. These two styles are slave morality and master morality. Slave morality includes fear of punishments while master morality relies on a strong will in interpreting individual situations. He claimed, "There are no moral phenomena at all, only moral interpretations of phenomena." How we interpret that phenomenon is the final decider of how we react. Many people look at manipulation negatively because of the historical connotation of the word. But stepping out of the slave morality of fear we experience manipulation for what it really is. Manipulation is causing behavior to occur. All incentivization is a form of manipulation.

Nietzsche was keyed in on the idea of a “will to power.” We must embrace our own ability to make things happen as we want and to fight against harmful events. He understood that “what is harmful to me is harmful in itself.” I must then work to ensure that the world is anything but harmful to me. I limit its ability to harm me, and I maximize my ability to benefit. To become the Übermensch I must self-actualize and give value to things/society rather than allow things/society to give value to me. I must take what I desire, rather than allow society tell me what to desire. In the paraphrased words of M.E. Thomas, I must stop conforming to the world around me and make it conform to me. I must manipulate it into what I want, and ensure I am not befuddled by what society tells me I should want. This takes an honest look at both society and myself. It takes study of who I am and where I find myself. Manipulation is a keystone to ensuring that I can effectively enact my own master morality. So how do I do that?

B. Manipulating Rules

It is important to understand that manipulation does not begin and end with manipulation of others. You must also become proficient at manipulating the rules. You do this in two real ways. Get existing rules to work for you or to change the rules in ways that benefit you. There are rules systems because flies love their rules, and with our mimic persona it is often easy to fit into the rule system as is. Ethics, morals, or just basic policy we can fit if needed. This allows for us to appear bipartisan in that we are just following rules, and are asking others to do the same. At times, though an opportunity comes about where we can change the rules. If it is safe to do so, then embrace that power. Remember though, just because you can, does not mean you should. Long-term goals might be hurt by the perception of unfairness those around you might have. The world wants us to conform to fairness. At times, it is better to conform rules to us. Which tactic is better, really depends on your situation. For now, let us assume you are fitting into a preexisting system.

Fitting into existing rules can take work, but with the correct persona in place you have this in the bag. Sorensen comments that sociopaths are often "amazingly successful people." And when we are "high functioning" we "are able to integrate successfully into society." I.e. in fly speak, we can follow the rules better than they can, and make those rules work for us to become "highly successful in any field they endeavor to join, both at work and in their personal lives. Sociopaths will go to extremes to excel, to the point that regular people would struggle to achieve the same heights." We see what it takes and do it. We make it a game and we win. Because we are winners.

This winning is not just in boring old what if's. It is best when the risks are great and the rewards are high. As M.E. glories in, "my excitement thrills more from mind games or intellectual pursuits where the reward-risk ratio is high." Where other humans get, nervous or find discomfort in high risk situations, we revel in them. The rules are there, we are playing the game, and on the 10-yard line we get to excel, where flies would choke.

The good news is that manipulating rules is easy. You first learn them. Get copies if they are written down. Ask what they mean by the people who have been following them for a long time. Understanding the letter of the law is the first step in understanding the spirit. You then simply create a persona of a rule follower. You fit into the system. The 10 Commandments are a good example of rules you can practice with. They are simple and already pervade our society. They cover a wide amount of behaviors and concentrate on those behaviors. The best part is that even most people within the system are not following all of them. When was the last time people followed the original Sabbath? Find simple rules and systems and practice them. This will help you learn to fit into more complex systems.

After knowing and fitting into a system the next step is to take control of the rules. Simple jobs like helping HR or joining committees are chances to effect what the future holds. Small local political offices and other volunteer work is a good step. You are out helping, and people see you positively for that.

The rules are important, we abide by them if they are expedient. Unfortunately for the flies the rules are not always expedient. Sometimes it may feel unfair that they stay on the marked path and we reach the finish line first because we cut over the grass, but life just is not fair. It is important at times to follow the rules as set. It is equally important to keep in mind rules are suggested behavior for success. If, like Alexander, success can come through cutting the Gordian Knot instead of untying it then that is what you need to do. You do not need to justify not following the suggestions of society. You just need to win. I know that this is not always fair to others, but the world is not fair, be aware of that. Face, it as a real fact. Just be cognizant that other people want the rules to be fair, so balance when you manipulate the rules with when you manipulate others. The flies' perception of fairness is often the downfall of spiders in completing our goals.

C. Manipulating Others

Manipulating others is the meat of this chapter. Controlling the narrative is the sauce, and manipulating rules are the bones. Sauce gives ribs the flavors you need to make them great. I use this analogy because rules give us shape, direction. Narrative control gives us the artistic ability to make life great, give it flavor. But let us face it without the right meat it all falls apart. You should be happy to pay extra for better meat. No additives, no hormones, grass fed, disgustingly delicious meat. Within the rules of your society and groups you will need to find ways to position people where you want them. This will be done in steps. First, calculate the value of people and their actions to you. Second, study the players on the board and the rules they are following which are effecting those values. Third, become the persona that fits the situation. Fourth, use your persona to push the players into position. Hence, exert your dominance, enjoy your place as the game master. Play the game until it achieves your goals or you need to get out. Lastly, learn to move forward without their incessant grasping holding you back. You can do this through complete destruction of the system you are leaving or through finding a replacement for your place in the game.

The first two parts are connected. You need to calculate

the value of people to your goals. This involves study of the players on the board. But really the first step is to calculate their value. Who are the important players? Who gets you were you need to be? Who can affect the perception you want to give off? Through study you can determine these groups. Do not ignore those that others over look. A secretary or assistant can have a hug impact on how you are perceived, and be hugely valuable with little work. In the Art of War the general Sun Tzu made it clear you need to understand the landscape you will fight upon. These first two steps are mapping that landscape.

In a corporation, knowing the rules that are in place and the people who have an impact on that landscape are important. Some people have more value than others. Find those people and discover what they desire in a persona. Fit into the rules, the corporate structure, and the culture. The culture of a business is vital to how the business runs. This is true for personal interactions as well as businesses but let us look at business for the ease of it. Once you understand who is valuable and who is not you can start to move forward with the seduction of the moment.

M.E. and myself call this a seduction because it is. You become the persona that fits with what they think they want. Embrace their needs, and supply their wants. Like a beau on a first date you shadow your negative attributes and highlight the things they desire in a worker/mate. You become the very essence of what a good employee/friend is to them. You will use mimicking here because it is part and parcel to the desired effect. If they like people that volunteer, then be that person. Give them the perfect person. You have it in you to become that person, so buy in. Seduce them, as you seduce any lover. The study you do of what they desire becomes your play book to the game.

Remember a few key points. People want to be led while not thinking they are led. Give them free reign after you have primed them to act as you desire. Do not micromanage their actions, but instead trust them. Trust is weird. You indoctrinate them into a specific view, and then let them follow it. Only adjusting as needed. They want to believe in free will, so let them. Further encourage people to vent to you. Become a secure confidant.

It is tough, because you do not really understand their frustrations. But, if you can encourage their open reliance you get insight into their needs while "connecting" to them in ways they want. You become the confessor of the company. The one person that is always on their side. This also opens the door for giving informal advice on behavior that can benefit you, or benefit them (the later ingratiates you). Sociopaths are hyper rational, you can see things they do not. You can suggest paths to them that will help them. So, help them. This is important, you must actually help them and benefit them. Ensuring their success will help ensure your own if they feel they owe you. Never blatantly call out that debt, but if needed subtly remind them with your own "venting." Some sociopaths attempt to own people through brute force. This may have its place, but let's face it those that want to help you are better than those that fear to not help you.

Side note, some people will hate you. You will just not be able to convince them you are the amazing person you are. At this point the study of who they want becomes a purer study of who they want you to be. If they want a villain, become a villain if it is efficient. Just do not go overboard there are still other people watching and judging. The real rule is to fit the mold of what they will react appropriately to. The constructs you created in the mimicking chapter will help here. You learned to frame and reference how they will react. You want specific reactions so begin to frame their perception to achieve those reactions. Remember this is an art, so you may need to adjust in the moment. The two rules in manipulation and mimicking is study and adaptability. Trust what you have laid out in your lists about what the landscape is, but be ready to adapt to changing times. Your goal is to push the players into places you want them in. This is like the game go, you reframe them in their own minds.

Once you have the study of everyone, the goals you desire, and you have become who they want you to be it is time for the next step. That step is to start positioning players where you need them. You are a player, so remember to position yourself as well as the others. You are playing the game. You seduce them into areas they want to be in, because it helps you to be where you want to be. It is best if everyone gets into positons they want, but that is not always possible. Still, you will want to ensure everyone feels like they won. This can mean you pretend to have lost, if it gets you where you want. Your study of the players and what they want is important to ensuring everyone feels like they won.

This can be done with incentives and punishments. The real rule here is to have clear expectations of people, and what they can achieve. They want to be led, and they have desires. Meet those desires. You have become who they want you to be. You have readjusted the landscape to fit your needs. Use that to help them, and they will help you. Cultural stories abound with deals that people make with "devils" to ensure their wants are met. Those that accept the deals are often seen as weak. You are the maker of the deal. Their weakness is your strength. You can get them a promotion in exchange for support. You can help with a personal project if it means it helps them accept your dominance, even if it is unknowingly to them. Do not be tied up with the idea of being the king, sociopaths are not Arthurs. We are Merlins. We are not tied down with ego and the need to rule, but only the need to dominate. Being behind the crown is more dominate, because you are making even the king your plaything. So, seduce a few candidates, and make a king. Better yet a queen, they are usually smarter and better at it.

At some point, you achieve your goals, and like any good sociopath you need to get out. You have milked the system and have made butter. The sad truth is we are all like children. We build a Lego tower to prove we can, and at that point we need to destroy the tower and start the next game. You know the players are about to expect what you cannot deliver. You are not a long term social grinder. You need an exit strategy. This is not as easy as it sounds, if you wish to continue a healthy lifestyle and successfully move on to the next manipulation. Whether you move up the ladder, or jump ladders, there will be complications. You have ingratiated yourself with those in the current manipulation group. You might need them again. You might not. Your options are to implode what you were and what was, or find ways for them to fill the void you are leaving. You do not and should never encourage them to hold on to the image that is you, which will be their desired step.

They will want to hold on to you. You are great why would they not? You fulfill all the things they want in a person. You are their confessor, their friend, their great leader, the love of their life. You are like two swimmers in the ocean treading water. There was a mutual benefit to holding onto each other, but now that the benefit is over there is only dead weight. Their insistent need to hold onto you will succeed only in dragging you both under the waves. You need your arms free to tread, and your legs free to kick. You both need to grow and change as people. But they just will not let go.

You need to successfully cut this lose. It will be tough because their mental minefield is not a thing you have ever internally dealt with. Because of this your instinctual response is to implode the relationships. Salt the earth, burn the fields implosion. But be careful. There are reasons this is a last resort. They will hold a grudge if you cause them pain. Just because you do not understand grudges does not mean they do not hold them. A grudge is a negative feeling they have that they hold onto until the feeling is appeased. Weird I know, but they have it. So be wary of it. You never know when they might have power you need in the future. So, implode the system only when you are completely free of any potential future repercussions. Otherwise try to coax them into letting go.

The best method of getting them to let go is to find a way to fill your spot, while making the separation feel like they desired it. Get a lover to break it off, or better yet insure they find another lover that takes your place. They will feel content with the ending, and like they owe you for leaving you for another. In business, help them pick a new manager, a manager you promise to support. At this point you have cut back your commitment from a whole group to one person. That person is gaining power and so owes you. You can then subtly suggest the issues they bring to you they should be able to handle without you. Subtle shame is important as a tool of manipulation, learn it. Those underneath the new manger (and hopefully the manger in question) will assume their failures are despite your assistance, and their successes are because of your help. This replacement method is best for all involved, and as stated earlier, manipulation is best, when everyone feels like it is a win-win. But at the end of the day you must learn to exit. The gentle approach is best. They are emotional creatures and their emotions can harm you if not mitigated. But regardless of how you exit, you must exit.

D. Practice

Let us conclude with the idea of practice. Every skill requires a place to practice. You have learned the rules, you may have even adjusted them. You have learned to study the landscape and assign value to all the people involved. You followed this up with positioning people, and playing the game, until you reached a point of completion. You then learned to replace yourself in these peoples live or to implode the entire system. Now that you are learning the basics, you must practice. We are not academics living in a pretend world. We are social philosophers, embracing the reality of the societies we live in. To practice you should find areas in which you can practice. Intramural sports or social groupings in other towns are a good start. Nonprofit groups not connected to anyone or anything you do are another. Embrace fringe groups that take little time to really delve into. Learn to study their group dynamic. These microcosms of humanity will give you chances to practice. If you are young join team sports, and other diverse groups to learn how groups interact. Learn a few roleplaying games to free your ability to practice manipulation. The goal here is to practice what you have learned, and to perfect your ability to shape a group to your needs.

Once joining a side group make a goal. Make it silly. Do not plan to take over. Instead plan another's path to ascension, or some other random idea you can make a goal. This gives you the freedom of learning how to shape a group without appearing to seek power. Seeking power for yourself is often the easiest way to be spotted. Ignore that desire in your practice, and instead, just make daily/weekly/monthly goals and work to achieve them. Things that have no impact on you. They just need your nudging to reach the goal. This practice will serve you well later in life, as you begin to use your manipulation skills to obtain real goals.

On a side note, sociopaths are not at heart liars, but lying is useful. I bring this up here because it is a good way to practice. I try two methods in my practice to ensure I get stronger. First, I pick a week where I refuse to lie. I have a challenge, and I must meet it. I must go that week without lying. I can withhold information, and I can talk around information, but I cannot lie. I make the conscious choice to become completely honest for this week. Like a saint, or a genie. I just cannot tell a lie. This helps me to strengthen my ability to shape narratives. Like in golf, any real handicap you give the other player helps you to become better, while keeping them weak. The second thing I do is pick a simple topic and never tell the truth about it. I make it silly, something that if caught out I will suffer no real consequences. I then lie about it. I make it a point to bring it up just to lie. I use this to test how far I can push the flies. They are gullible, but I need to practice my lying to improve it. Poker and other games of deceit are good for this as well, you are encouraged to practice lying in these games so play them. We are not at heart liars. It is often more expedient to tell the truth. But we must practice the arts of truth and lies to ensure that we can use which ever tool is needed.

In conclusion manipulation requires you to understand how to control the narrative. You must begin to learn to highlight what you want others to see, and shadow what they should not. You improve your narrative through manipulating rules. First, by embracing the rules that are there. Second, by learning to change the rules to your benefit. And lastly, by remembering rules are suggestions that at times you can ignore to win. You combine rule manipulation with the manipulation of others. You assign value to players. You study the landscape and players. You create a persona the current system wants. You position everything as you need it, and play the game until you reach a point of winning. You then leave the game, by either destroying what is or by replacing yourself as a player. All of this is important to learn, and so you practice in small groups to ensure you understand the whys and how's of what you are doing. You are a sociopath, a spider, manipulation is your legacy. Embrace it. And it will serve you well.

Chapter Six:

Disconnected

Sociopaths have no emotional connection to the world around them. We come across as glib and superficial because for us everything is superficial. We are glib because there is humor to be found everywhere. The worst pain is best survived through humor. Everything is better enjoyed if you join it with laughter. Why be sorrowful of things or take them seriously when you can have fun with them. The best goal of life is to let go and have fun, so it is odd to me that this is counted against us. We are disconnected. The existentialists embraced this idea that the world was without any real meaning beyond what we give it. The basis of their ideas that the universe is at its heart meaningless was a look deep into the soul of sociopaths. We are born to see the world in a constant state of existential crises. A state the flies experience in short bursts and then run away from. Camus with his idea of absurdity is an informative example. Experiencing the world as absurd causes sociopaths to appear glib.

We are disconnected from ourselves as can be seen in behavior that others see as self-destructive or dangerous. We see it as searching after experiences. Both our impulsive need to act and our obsessive focus on things can put us in danger that others just cannot understand because they are attached to the status quo. We have no self, we understand there is nothing to be attached to. I may face pain and suffering for my actions, but they are my actions. I am driven in ways that others do not understand because the joy they can receive from the action is overridden by fear and emotional panic that holds them back.

We are also disconnected from the world around us including others. What others feel or think is not our business and we struggle to understand why it should matter to us. When other people experience pain, we are expected to sympathize with it. But why, how is this sharing even possible. I have no way of knowing what you are feeling or if that feeling is even real. I am expected to be held back by guilt when my actions possibly cause suffering. This idea is alien to me. I am responsible only for myself. Why must I be equally responsible for how others feel? I am absent emotion, and no one takes that into account in dealing with me. Yet society determines that I must consider that they are emotional. It is lopsided.

The flies are so needy. I look at them and I can only see the painful hooks their eyes are trying to apply to my mind. There is this their weakness diving into me. It is a yearning they have that is pulling at me. It irritates and drains me at the same time. They just have so many needs that they seem to believe can be fixed externally. They are broken, and they will never be fixed because they refuse to look at the one thing in the world that can fix them, themselves. They are weak because they refuse to empower themselves. They wonder why we perceive them in such negative ways. Why we have no respect for them. Their weakness is their business. It is disgusting that they try to force those emotions onto us. They try to dig down and bury them inside us. They hate us because they cannot force us to take on their pain.

The existentialist Camus discussed the need to embrace the absurdity of the world through the creation of our own personal made up value systems. Camus said that all humans if lucky will reach a point of existential crises where they realize that the world is meaningless, and their place in it more so. It is a deep pit for Camus, this place where all Sociopaths live. He believed the normal human could never live here indefinitely and the mind would make one of three choices.

The first reaction, which Camus thought was the most logical though least desirable, was suicide. The fact that the world was meaningless meant there was no reason to live with in it. It was logical to just end the façade of meaning with death. The second option, which for Camus was slightly worse and less logical, was to just live with it. Experience the daily pain of having no meaning. For him it was a hollow existence of just plugging along at life in a state of absurd suffering because humans require meaning. The third reaction, which Camus subscribed for himself as the best option if not the most logical, was to become a Don Quixote of meaning. He said that we should create our own meaning. For Camus things like beauty, justice, and truth could be created and held onto as personal meanings for his existence.

He likened it to Sisyphus pushing the rock constantly up the hill. You see Sisyphus was cursed to push a rock up a mountain every day cursed to never reach the top. At some point before reaching the pinnacle his curse would roll the rock back down to the bottom. He would then be forced to start again. His curse created a constant meaningless duty toward an end that had no purpose. But Camus said that Sisyphus was most pure at that moment he watched the rock reach the bottom and he chose to walk back down and start again. He embraced his meaningless existence and decided to still chose to keep going in his pointless endeavor. Better yet he gave his own meaning to his constant struggle.

Camus had some great points, and will always be in my top five philosophers to read. But the sociopath sidesteps Camus' angst at the moment of crisis. Sociopaths do this because we cannot lie to ourselves and create fake attachments to the world. We constantly face the realization of meaninglessness, and for us there is no escape. But for us, we are built to live free. Where the flies have option three, and the ability to believe for a time the fake attachments through imagined meanings the spiders do not. We never make a choice, because we are not attached to the idea of meaning.

We go about our lives seeing the absurd and experiencing it. But we are lucky in that we also do not understand emotional suffering. We embrace this existence through disconnection from ourselves and others. We see the world through clear eyes and so we function very well in the abyss of absurdity and meaninglessness. We are born without the need to find meaning. Honestly the very idea of a meaning to life seems alien and unnatural to me. I was created without the need to understand. Sure, we like to understand, but living entire lives without understanding anyone around us gives us a unique perspective. We would not be able to comprehend the idea of meaning and connection even if we experienced it. We are born with an inability to connect to the world around us or even to ourselves. If anything, we face the opposite of the existential crises. There is a tension in that other people try to force us to feel connections that they imagine. For us the tension is not in trying to find meaning but trying to live surrounded by people that believe that meaning exists.

To better understand ourselves we must look at how we are disconnected from ourselves and how we are disconnected from others. What this means and how we embrace and focus it for the benefit of functioning in society.

a. Self

There is a famous story found in ancient writing about a king of Persia. This king was newly minted to his rule after taking over from his father and he understood that to rule he needed wisdom he did not have. He gathered all the wise folk of his time into one room and asked them to find him that wisdom. His demand was a single phrase that would give him hope in times of loss and drive him to further greatness even in times of plenty. The stories change here. Some say the group came together to create the phrase. Others claim they failed and one old man came forward with the wisdom required. All the stories agree though that an answer was found. They created a phrase and emblazoned it on a single silver ring they gifted to the king. The phrase was, “thus too shall pass.” The king was skeptical but he put on the ring and went about his business.

He became a great king, and ruled justly. As happens when one is successful, his neighbors envied his rich and prosperous kingdom so they decided to take it. He went to war. In one great battle, he faced insurmountable foes and lost. He hid in the bushes with a few elite soldiers and he despaired. Within his despair the ring felt heavy on his finger so he looked up on it and realized that this suffering, this would pass. He had been great, and now he hid in bushes as armies marched on his kingdom, but this failure would pass. He embraced that ideal and rallied his troops. He worked hard to lead them to a great victory against the forces of his enemies and bested them. He conquered city after city, uniting the middle east under him. He was faced with how to assimilate these new conquests into his kingdom. Again, the ring weighed upon his finger and looking at the phrase he realized, thus too shall pass. His greatness was not forever. His kingdom was not forever. He had won the day, but what about tomorrow when his enemies might take what he had won. Against the advice of those that told him to annihilate all those that stood against him he showed compassion. He gave them freedom and a happy life under his rule. He understood that what he held today, he would/could one day lose.

This king realized the one truth that all sociopaths are born with, "thus too shall pass." Who I am and what I have today will be gone tomorrow. It is best to embrace the now and enjoy it and live life as we find it. The king felt no need to bully when he could make friends or despair when he had none. He knew that what he had rested on him, and so he did what he could to maximize his benefit from it until it was gone. Because all we are will one day be gone. The need to suffer from our current state, or glory in our current success is absurd. It will all pass. Grasping at a connection with who I see myself as now is a recipe for disaster. The Buddha later summed it up in the four noble truths that craving and grasping are nothing but ineffectual attempts to hold onto something stable in an unstable world. It is best to embrace that instability and seek after your current desires.

Sociopaths are lucky in that we do not suffer from this attachment to the self. I can be a politician at the top of her game today, and a vagabond traveling the world the next. To hold onto what is now into what will be is a disaster in the waiting. It is best to be the wind and let it all pass through you. You have no self. You have no core. You are only your will and desires. Meet them, accomplish the goals as needed, and move forward.

Being risk averse is counterproductive to innovation. You believe you risk yourself, but really you only risk the image you have of you. Embrace the chaos. You are not your possessions. You are not your image. You are not your health and safety. You are your will and drive that exists right now. The best thing you can do is embrace that. Society tries to tell the sociopath to hold to that image of themselves they have. Society is wrong. You need to be free. You need to take risks regardless of consequences. You are a spider and at times you need to jump without looking for the next landing. You are a mask with nothing inside that mask, an act without an actor, what are you really risking?

Your disconnection from your Self is a positive and a strength. It allows you to give in to the impulses to act that you feel, without fear of repercussions of the consequences. Dr. Hare when studying sociopaths used an interesting method to find us before his checklist according to the book The Psychopath Test by Jon Ronson. He would bring in prisoners and tell them he was going to shock them. He would then shock the fuck out of them. They would scream and cry, and feel so much pain. He would stop, and tell them he was going to go again. And he would go again. He would do this over and over while the prisoner was attached to an MRI.

What he found was that flies had all this pre-mental tension about what was about to happen. They suffered before there was suffering due to anticipation. Their self was about to be hurt and they suffered at the thought of it. But sociopaths, well those prisoners had no pre-mental worry. They knew it was coming. They prepared their bodies as best they could. But there was no apprehension, no fear, no worry, just acceptance. They knew they were at a state of being that was going to change. That state of being would change back. And really who cared. They had that moment to do the best they could.

There was a disconnect in their brains that allowed them to accept the change that was coming without fear. Every time someone asks me if I am excited or worried about a trip or test I understand what the prisoners went through. I have no anticipation of the change. When the change happens, I accept the change. Until then I live with the current status quo. I plan and prep for what is next, but I do not feel anything about it. I just know it is coming and react accordingly. I have travelled the world and jumped from planes all with no internal dialogue about it other than, “this is about to happen you need to react accordingly.” I can step into a court of law and try a major case with no real qualms. I have no connection with my current state of being, so I am free to change and risk it as needed. This is intertwined yet separate from my complete disconnection from others.

b. Others

Let me be honest I have no connection to you. I see you laugh or cry and feel no need to join you. I am not sure that what you feel is even real. I often must hide this. It creates discomfort in others to know that I just do not feel any empathy for what they are feeling. It pains those around me and confuses them. They expect connection. They assume they are not special to me because I just do not care, but the truth is no one is special unless I find value in them. And even those that are special I just cannot be bothered to care about. The emotional states of others are a weakness in my eyes. They suffer only in their minds and that is weird. I understand my feelings, they are limited, why must I strive to understand other people's? I find the constant pushing on me to feel something a distraction and irritant. The world would do better to just free themselves from this burden. The flies around me bombard me with attempts to grasp at my being. If you are a fly and know a sociopath do him/her a favor and lighten up. Let them be them.

Cleckley railed against sociopaths' lack of recognizing a reality he found that, "so obviously existed." But why is it obvious? This inner world of others he found so obvious as to be apparent to all. The inner world of others is anything but obvious.

Just as Wittgenstein found when discussing the beetle in the box scenario. I have no idea that what you feel is real, or if it is, what it might be. Wittgenstein outlined a scenario where in we each are holding boxes. You look in your box and see a beetle. You ask what is in my box. I tell you, it has six legs, a hard shell covering wings, antae, etc. I describe the thing in my box to such a degree you liken it to the beetle in your own. We use words to communicate that creature we call beetle, but do you know I have a beetle? Do you know that what is in my box is what is in your box? No, you can never know. Because only I can see what is mine, and only you can see what is in yours. We are trapped in this unique view we each have and find communication only important in being able to trade ideas.

I am trapped in my own world, and you are trapped in your own world. I can predict or even push you to certain actions, but I will never understand what is in your mind. What is in your box. We are trapped in a disconnected framework that we are both attempting to make sense of. The difference between spiders and flies are that we spiders do not assume a connection between our boxes. Mine is mine and yours is yours. Spiders understand that there will never be a bridge beyond this moment. I can never communicate to you what is truly in my mind, and neither can you. Why fight it. Why attempt a bridge, when what we have is enough? We can both find joy and pleasure in shared experience, even if the True experience will never be shared. Why must I empathically feel what you feel for us to find joy in our moment. Why must there be a connection? The flies beg for it. They lie to themselves that they experience it. But really my experience is mine. I do not expect you to share it, nor should you. We are equally open to the experiences we are creating. That should be enough.

The normal fly goes beyond wanting this experience of connection and they feel emotional panic over the lack there of. They feel connection to a self and a social group, and breaching those ideas causes them to react in insane ways. The lack of emotional panic will be covered in Hyper Rationality, but it is important to understand that their imagined connection to the world is what causes it. They imagine a self, they imagine empathy with others. When this is threatened, they feel such a strong discomfort they panic over it. They cannot accept the world is different from what they perceive so they grow tense and angry and act out. Sociopaths do not experience this, because there is no self or outer world to grasp on to. There is only the desires of now. And now is all that is important.

This chapter covered our disconnection from the self and others. We went over the existential crisis's realization that there is no meaning. We embraced the idea that we are free from such constructs as we live within an absurd world that just keeps on moving on. We embraced the lack of connection to a real self as we have no self, and only the illusionary image of that self exists. We further looked at the disconnection from others. Through Wittgenstein we learned that there is no way to ever know if there is another, or if what they feel is even real. Sociopaths in this specific framework are free to act however benefits them because there are no other actors that exist metaphysically speaking. Sociopaths are the wind, and everything else passes through them. The weight of others attempting to grasp them may weigh heavily, but in the end, they just float away like leaves. Flies experience emotional panic due to their imagined connection with themselves and others. The hyperrationality often attributed to sociopaths is due to this lack of connection, and freedom from unnecessary grasping at illusionary beliefs about reality. We are the wind, and you pass through us.

Chapter Seven:

Hyper Rational

Sociopaths are often attributed to have heightened intelligence and utilize a mental system of hyperrationality in comparison to normal people. Both in fiction and reality sociopaths are perceived to be able to see things that others cannot, and learn things above their standard ability. Fictional characters such as Sherlock Holmes or Hannibal Lector are seen as making connections that others cannot. In Cleckley's examples of patients he makes constant reference to sociopaths with little or no formal education that wrote and spoke at a PhD level when it benefited them. They performed complex jobs well above what they should have been able to understand without more technical education then they had. But what is the cause of this image we have garnered throughout the decades? Why are we capable of appearing so much more intelligent than the flies? The Buddha said, "Know well what leads you forward and what holds you back, and choose the path that leads to wisdom." In this chapter, we will begin to discuss the attribute of hyper rationality found in sociopaths and how we can embrace this strength.

Though it is true sociopaths are often smarter than their counterparts, the image of highly intelligent sociopaths is not due to an inherently more advanced IQ. Instead it can be contributed to a more efficient system of interacting with our perceptions. Like Socrates in ancient Greece by perceiving the world devoid of preconceived ideas we can make connections that other people cannot. This out of the box thinking allows leaps of thought other people find difficult. Thomas in her own story talks about her lack of the same expectations of others leading her to be capable of great insights. Flies are held back by the constant internal voice telling them what they should expect to perceive; or that they will fail, get caught, get hurt, be laughed at. A constant internal negative reinforcement. Sociopaths lack that voice, and can push ahead with an openminded worldview.

This open-minded policy is available to sociopaths because like the Scottish empiricist David Hume we understand that all our knowledge is gathered strictly from experience. One can only truly claim knowledge about what can be experienced. Seeing as most human perception is flawed, that knowledge is necessarily flawed. Sociopaths may not inherently understand this, but we exemplify it by living it. We are devoid of the rose-colored glasses of emotion and attachment that other humans are restricted by.

Hume further went on to discuss ethics as formed from

feelings and emotions rather than any rational exercise. Sociopaths being absent emotions are therefore absent the Hume based ethical codes others have. Our disconnection from others and our lack of emotions work together to ensure we never experience the emotional panic that cause others to act in illogical ways. We are free to see the logical paths because we are not tied down by emotions.

Sociopaths are often unstable. Finding stabilizing forces in our lives that can use our hyper rationality is important to ensure it is used at its most effective. A person that understands what we are, or at least how to manage things for us is a good step. Jobs such as consulting, lawyer, or problem solving specialists that allow short term evaluations and tasks before moving on are a good way to maximize the benefits of our abilities while minimizing some of our negatives. One of the great weaknesses of the sociopath is in our impulses to act out and our obsessions that develop during times of boring repetitive behavior, which can lead to highly unstable consequences. Mitigating those consequences is an important step to functioning. To enjoy all the benefits of our hyper rational abilities we must have plans in place to utilize them.

To fully grasp why sociopaths are considered to have such a high intelligence it might be good to look at the human considered to be the wisest of them all. Socrates was an ancient Athenian that spent his days wandering to and fro questioning those in the city. His questionings were recorded by multiple sources but none so thoroughly as his pupil Plato. By all accounts Socrates was undeniably a smart guy (a bit annoying but smart), but what made him so wise? The Oracle once told the world that Socrates was the wisest man in the world because he understood that he knew nothing. This was the key to his ability to see things clearly; he had no preconceived ideas holding him back. He came at a problem assuming he did not know the answer. His questioning of others and himself flowed without the hindrance of attachment to the answers.

Sociopaths likewise are unhindered by emotional baggage and attachment to the answers they are looking for. When asking questions, they are free to hear or reach any answer that is available. Emotional attachment to what they want or think the answer to be holds back the normal person from finding the best answer. The search for what is "right" inhibits them from finding what is best. This blindness is absent from sociopaths. Professor Joseph Newman's research makes the claim that sociopaths are experiencing all the same input as normal people, we just cannot see things others focus on. We are free then to spot those things others would miss. For Professor Newman, this is a "mind-blindness" of sociopaths, but our inability to attach value to what we are seeing is far from a blindness. Because we do not assume a thing has value, we are free to see everything there is to see about it. We come to the table like Socrates, meaning we know we nothing, and so we are free to learn what is there to learn. Because of this we can embrace "out of the box" thinking that so many other humans struggle with.

Emotions and attachments hold back the mental abilities of flies in many ways. Of course, as discussed above there is the subtle blindness to not seeing specific things. But let us face it their emotions and internal dialogue do more than just keep them from seeing the world as it really is. This voice talks them out of being who they could be. A key example is the internal negative voices that all flies seem to have. They have this internal negative reinforcement telling them what they cannot accomplish. They want to try out for a new job they hear a constant dialogue of how they will never get it. They get the job and they constantly tell themselves they are not worthy of it, or they cannot do it. They have all kinds of terms about how they self-sabotage.

Sociopaths never have this voice, we have no voices other than those we create. A sociopath can walk into any room and start doing the job. Not because they have the skills or abilities needed, but because they do not have a fear to try. There are stories of sociopaths so buying into their persona of the moment that they land planes and perform surgery all without training. Now I am not one to suggest anyone should try such a thing. Succeed or fail those sociopaths ended up in jail for trying. But the point is they so lacked that negative nagging voice, so they tried. They were like the genetically defunct brother in Gattaca, swimming past the point of no return because he never bothered to hold anything back. He lacked the voice that told him he could not do it. It gave him the drive to make the attempt, the ability to succeed. It makes him dangerous to himself and others through lack of internal restrictions. It also opens doors only spiders realize are open. It allows us to be daring in the face of danger, and obstinate in the face of loss. We do not fear to lose, so we push through often into the win.

This lack of attachments and reliance on empirical knowledge stem from how sociopaths interact with our world and our perception of it. The skeptic David Hume outlined how knowledge is gained by humans through perception. There are only two forms of knowledge for Hume, Impression and Ideas. Impressions are immediate perceptions/experiences in the moment, while Ideas are reflections on those impressions. A perception of remembering a perception if you will. In this all we can ever know is based from those perceptions. Now we can abstract the ideas into combinations of interesting ideas but none of the ideas are new, just new combinations.

Because of human knowledge's reliance on perception it is necessarily flawed. You see human perception is flawed. Hume uses examples such as an oar halfway into the water that appears to be bent. This and other examples can be looked at to understand just how flawed our perceptions of the world are. This flaw reflects onto our knowledge, as one cannot create perfection from flaws. For Hume, we cause further flaws in this knowledge by building assumptions such as cause and effect. We assume that the series of actions that occur today will be the order in which they always occur. We assume that because the sunrises and sets today it will rise and set again tomorrow. It will follow the same path and be caused by the same actions in the universe. We throw a ball and it flies forward striking another ball knocking it forward. Most people work off the mistaken assumption that they know for a fact that every time they throw that ball the same thing will happen. Why is this? Because it is assumed that one action caused the other, and so always will. But Hume made clear that there is no proof of this assumption. We make up some of our assumptions and we learn others from those around us. But all these assumptions add a second layer of flaws.

Sociopaths are recognizably at an advantage in this system. It is not that we can magically perceive the world without the rose-colored glasses of perception. We are just as trapped in flawed impressions feeding into flawed ideas as the next human. This first layer of flaws we share with the flies. We break the cycle leading to the next layer though in two main ways. First, we fail to make the same assumptions that others make, and second when taught those assumptions by others we largely ignore them whenever we desire. If the sun were to fail to rise tomorrow. Most of the flies would freak out. But not the spiders, the spiders would mark it as something new and keep moving forward. We are not trapped in unproven and unprovable assumptions because of our disconnection and apathy. We may then be trapped behind the first layer of flawed perception, but we are free from the second layer that traps other people.

Hume was not all logic and reasonable ideas built from perception though. He also spoke about ethics. For Hume, there was no rational cause for ethical beliefs. Instead he believed that a feeling of wrongness towards certain behaviors and actions ensured we acted in a way that was considered "good" or bad." Ethics then were based on emotions and emotional reactions to things we experience. From my experience watching the flies and their ethical dilemmas all mixed up with their emotions I can only conclude that he is correct in his assertions here. The flies seem to develop ethical codes based purely on the fact that certain behaviors affect them emotionally in negative and positive ways. They then build ethical codes from the ground up to justify these beliefs. When unable to rationally justify the rules though they can always relax into the comforting arms of religion and morality. Why think it through when you can just embrace a myth. When faced with an event outside of these rationalizations and assumptions the flies fall back on the one guiding principle of their lives, emotion.

Emotion is the defining characteristic of the flies. They are driven by it, and controlled by it. These controlling drives are so intertwined in their core selves that the flies attribute the lack of emotion as the spider's main attribute. As if the lack of a thing could be the defining characteristic of a thing. But regardless they have them, and we do not. If something negatively impacts them they often react with what sociopaths like to refer to as emotional panic. When faced with situations that cause emotional responses the flies react in highly emotional ways that cause them to exhibit what appear to be insane actions. A prime example of this are when faced with a large load of work. Many flies will be overcome by the sheer amount, and so in an emotional panic they do nothing. They find reasons to procrastinate, put off that which needs done. They react highly irrationally, and incomprehensibly to those of us that do not experience emotions. They live these lives controlled by an imaginary connection to other things, and how those connections make them feel. How horrible it must be.

But even with all these benefits to our worldview sociopaths can be highly unstable. It is important for sociopaths to find stability. Our hyper rationality gives us many advantages over the flies, but our disconnection from ourselves and impulse to act often drives us to unstable behavior. Just because we can see the world in ways that others cannot does not mean we can always be bothered to follow through with the plan. Why should we, in that moment, a different impulse is more important. But there have been functioning sociopaths that utilized stabilizing forces in their lives to minimize their instability and maximize their hyper rationality. Cleckley spoke to one patient who had spent most of his life running a very successful business. The business had started to fail and his family was worried. Upon researching the patient, it was discovered he had had a partner for years. The partner provided stability while the patient had provided the insight into how to run the business. Much like Dr. Watson is for Holmes, the partner smoothed over the sociopath's more eccentric behavior.

This is a key lesson in going beyond functioning and beginning to become successful in the society of the flies. We are smarter than they are. We see a clearer world, unencumbered by all these uncomfortable emotions, and silly commitments to sillier assumptions. But these only benefit us if we use them. We need to find stabilizing factors in our world that can use these gifts. We can use a partner such as the patient above to counteract our instability and cover for us when we go off on an adventure. We can choose jobs that maximize our unique ability to process the world while minimizing our inability to take it seriously for long periods. I have seen sociopaths successfully go into jobs such as consulting, attorney, some forms of problem solvers, non-profit, etc. Anything that allows short term commitments coupled with a way to show off your strengths.

Hyper rationality is an important attribute that all sociopaths share. How well they use that attribute is up to their individual skill. Some of us practice and some of us are naturally smarter. These things add up to some us being better equipped than others. We naturally appear to have a heightened intelligence in comparison to non-sociopaths but this is often since we are free from preconceived ideas. We embrace the stance of Socrates in understanding that we begin every moment not knowing anything. We benefit from this in being able to see the world much more open minded. We further have no internal voice telling us what we should see or cannot do. Instead we embrace our ability to try anything, living fearlessly, without the emotional baggage flies experience.

Much of this is tied to how humans garner knowledge. Scotsman David Hume explained that knowledge comes from perceptions and experiences. These perceptions are flawed, and so is the knowledge based off them. Sociopaths benefit by not adding another layer of mistaken ideas over the perceptions in the way that flies do. We instead embrace that we do not have knowledge of the world beyond the now.

The flies further create their ethics from emotional states of being that they are driven to follow. Failure to accept reality for what it is often leads them to succumb to emotional panic. The world is filled with things that just do not fit with their assumptions and desires, and so they react irrationally. Learning to live around this constant mewling is important to become functioning. But not as important as learning to overcome your own instability and take advantage of your strengths. You are strong, you just need to embrace your great parts and focus your weaknesses.

Chapter Eight:

Self-Centric

As a sociopath, I am at my core self-centric. I understand that there are other people, but I have a hard time connecting with them or seeing them as real actors instead of objects to fulfill my needs. Spiders are naturally solitary creatures that have a very strong sense of territory and ownership. This might sound odd, I mean I have no self, so how can I be self-centric? I recognize that I may have no self, but I do have drivers and desires. By being self-centric I concentrate on my own driver and my own desires above those of others. The philosopher Immanuel Kant separated things in the world into ends and means. Some things he recognized as being both, and I assume he would recognize that somethings are neither. What he thought though is that rational beings must always be an end. It was unethical in his view to ever treat a rational being as a means. Now there is debate on whether he meant only humans, or if as we learn more about the world we can expand his idea of rational being. I have also heard the debate that it should apply to all feeling creatures. These debates to me are gibberish. You see I am my own end. I am only my end, I am not your end, I am mine.

You should be your end. If we all seek our own self betterment, we will work together to make a better world.

I pride myself on being goal orientated, and I firmly believe that my goals are the only goals. The goals of others are tools to reach my own, but if the other person fails to obtain their goals, it is because they failed. It is not my place or my business how they define their success or how they reach it. This does not mean I fail to pay attention to the needs of others, on the contrary. A well run and happy society benefits me. When the water rises so do all boats. I am more than happy to help others, sometimes even at short-term detriment to myself. I want those around me to be happy, it makes things easier for me. But if they fail in their happiness, I have no reason to feel guilty. We all have our wits about us. I expect you to use yours. In these group settings, I want everyone to get what they want, but it behooves me to be the dominate party. By being near the top, I can better manage my wants and needs. I have more leeway in finding opportunity and limiting tragedy. I have no real capacity to love as other people do, but this does not preclude me from forming bonds in my own way. I can take on a sense of ownership of a person or persons, and their needs become important to me.

The first step in understanding and focusing your attribute of self-centrism is the idea that sociopaths understand the reality that there is no self. The disconnection we feel with everything includes the self as it does others. If I fail at a task, or end up on the street I am as content as if I am setting in a nice house with all my goals met. I can win or lose this game and it is all the same to me, because for me it is all a game. And yet I have desires that I want met. I am driven to meet those desires. I want to enjoy a moment or an object, so I work to achieve it. If I reach it or fail to reach it makes no matter. I am still driven to obtain my goal when I can. Obtaining my goals has a feeling I enjoy. A feeling of winning. That feeling is often as important as the actual object of my desire.

Before moving into Kant, we should note that in his duty based theory that requires one to have a good will, as he defines it, sociopaths will never have the good will he requires. The deontological system he has created with the categorical imperative is completely out of the sociopath's reach. But this side note is one of many, and the discussion of the ends and means is much more important to illuminate how a sociopath sees the world. In the philosophy of Immanuel Kant, we see the distinction between things he terms as ends and things he calls means. An end is a reason in itself. One can think of ends as the goal, but it goes deeper than that. I am the end. I am the goal/objective. There are many types of ends in the world, and we work to achieve them. The way we reach ends is through means. Means are things used to obtain ends. Such as I use a sandwich to fulfill my need to be full. I and my full state of being then is the end, the sandwich and eating it are the means. The sandwich was and end while I was creating it, but mostly it and its creation were a means.

Kant goes further though to say all rational beings are only ends. For him you, by the magical state of being able to think, are an end and never a mean. It becomes unethical in a Kantian perspective for you to ever be treated as a mean. To use an example. "I want a beautiful lover I can show off," is for Kant an unethical desire. Because the lover in question will be (I slightly assume) a human rational being. My statement by its nature treats the lover as a mean to an end. I have a goal, and to reach it I need to use another person the way I used my sandwich above. This for Kant is never acceptable.

Kant goes into a lot of strict rules and regulations based around both this ends-means debate and his categorical imperative (logic and duty based ethics). But the issue we are discussing here is the duty he feels we have toward every rational being to treat them as an end and only an end. Obviously as a sociopath I have an inherent disconnect from his view. I am an end, I am my own end. I further see you as your own end. There are billions of humans on this planet, and once you start adding all other life the number becomes unimaginable. Side note, if I was not a sociopath I would likely be some type of gross vegan. I mean why are humans special here? We are all animals, so to apply a rule to one of us, logically speaking it should be applied to us all.

But I digressed. You are your own end. I am my own end. If I was worried about every other end out there I would spend my day not achieving any of my goals. Pure efficiency demands that I focus on my own desires, and my own self as an end. If I assume that you will be doing the same, we will work together to compromise into a solution that works for us all. It is not my business what you think of me or my goals. It is not my business what you want or how you want to achieve them. What I worry about is your wants impact on me, and how I can use that and you to achieve my goals. Every day I use other people.

A core attribute of what we are is the need to manipulate, and the perfection of that becomes an art form that we can revel in. The idea at play for sociopaths is much more like Adam Smith and the invisible hand. If we are all working toward our own rational self-interest, we can live in an ever-changing world of competition based economic prosperity. I know Kantians will argue, but Smith's system has worked as capitalism for a very long time, while Kant's ideas struggle from over developed stricture and hard to force duty. I must admit, if Kant is correct then I am unethical. His idea of duty to others and logical ethics is incomprehensible to a sociopath in its natural form. I do agree that I live in a world where my ethical structure is semi duty based. But my duty is not to others, it is not even to myself. My duty is to my desires. Which I obtain through my goals and actions.

I am goal orientated. I think it is a great world where people create goals and work to achieve them. My goals though are the only goals. I understand that others have goals, and I pay attention to that. But they are a means to reaching my goals. If that means I help them in getting what they want, then awesome. If they instead fail and end up in a ditch, well, boohoo. Their failure is their own and none of my business. I am fully apathetic to their failure. This includes if I actively cause their failure as a stepping stone to my own success. We played a game, they should have played better. They had a duty to themselves which they ignored.

All of this said being self-centric requires I pay attention to the needs of others. M.E. Thomas was correct in asserting that sociopaths benefit from a well-run society in which everyone gets what they want. Treating manipulations as win-win situations ensures we can double dip from previously used wells. When we harm those around us or leave bad tastes in the mouths of those we have used then it is unlikely we will be able to use them again in the future. Like a good lover, you are more likely to continue to have your wants met if everyone involved leaves satisfied. This means do the best you can to meet your needs while limiting how you damage those around you. By working to ensure everyone is happy you help to ensure your own happiness. Many assume that being self-centric means I am out to hurt others, but really, I cannot be bothered to hurt others unless it serves a purpose. And honestly it is often so much easier and materially rewarding to help people.

This is helped by our lack of connection to self and our impulse to act. I have many times on a whim given away what to me meant nothing but to the flies who received my largesse meant more than I can even understand. They have a connection to material goods I never will, so the lose return ratio for me is calculated differently. They feel this tension of owing me. I do not feel like they owe me, but at the end of the day they do. That feeling they have puts me in their good graces, makes future manipulations easier, and ensures my future whims are met. I become the dominate force in their life through my nice behavior. And dominance is a major driver in my life.

Dominance is an interesting feeling. Sociopaths naturally

crave power and dominance. And why should we not? It feels good to be the alpha. It feels good to have an alpha who can lead and be strong for us. Alphas give direction. A good alpha ensures the entire pack's needs are met. They take care of the weak members, and in return reap the benefits of dedicated followers. Being the dominate member of a group creates a duty to protect what is yours (the other members), but it is a tradeoff. By being dominate you have leeway to ensure your success. For example, being dominate means that when opportunities arise you are in place to take advantage of them. You have the power and the means to use those opportunities to meet goals, and a clear system in place to create new opportunities. Further when negative events transpire you are more capable of handling them. With a dedicated following you can face those tragedies more easily. You have a line of defense between you and your mistakes to ensure set backs are only momentary. This dedicated following attached to being dominate builds from our sense of ownership of those we dominate. They want to be owned. Without the capacity to love this sense of ownership is all we have as a tool to really connect with others.

Sociopaths are unable to love. It is a fact. We have feelings and behaviors that we call love. But it is not love, not as the flies experience it. We are pathologically egocentric with a complete disconnection from other people. But we can in the correct circumstances find a connection through ownership. They become our group, our people, our objects. This connection creates the need to protect them and benefit them similar as to what we do for our ourselves. I take great care of my car, amazing care of my house, and even greater care of those that become part of my social group. I feel like they are mine, and so I work to ensure that what I have is the best it can be. My lover needs the best of everything. They represent me, they need to be amazing. I make friends with amazing people, or I make sure my friends begin to live amazing lives. They are extensions of and representations of me. My house needs to be the best house, with the best plants and care. My humans are no different. I buy them things, and encourage them to make and obtain goals. I want to point and say, "that is mine" with pride. I may not be able to feel true love, but I can feel a source of ownership that equates to the same thing, and often leaves them better off than if I had merely loved them.

The best method of understanding our self-centric attribute is to understand it's parts, the ideas around it and how it applies in the real world. Being self-centric does not imply I look out for myself because I have no self to look out for. What it does mean is that I have desires and reaching my desires should come before anything else. This is explored through Kantian views of means and ends and how they conflict with the ideas of Adam

Smith. It allows us to focus on being goal orientated and ensuring that our goals are the only goals that matter. It is true we at times assist others in obtaining their goals, but their goals are their business. Their failure or success in reaching them lies with them, and I must look towards obtaining my own. That said looking out for my own interests means I often need to look out for the interests of others. Either through a system of quid pro quo, symbiotic goals, or simply banking for the future; I understand that helping them meet their goals has the potential to help me. This also fills my need to be dominate. I can ensure my dominance and the dedication of my group through 'selfless' acts towards group members. I am driven to be dominate, and these acts ensure my power and standing in the group. I further encourage this as the group members become mine. This feeling of ownership replaces my feelings of love. I can connect with them and increase my own image by improving and protecting those things that help make up my image. This can stretch from taking care of my beautiful home to having my friends find their own success. In the end, I am a solitary creature that only cares about itself. I find that my desires are paramount to all other things. I accept that and embrace it. I find ways to ensure my own success is assured.

Chapter Nine:

Driven by a Need to Act

The last two chapters in this section go over drivers of ours that do not always work together. They are in fact often in tension with each other, and yet when they work together they are unstoppable forces driving us. These chapters go over two of the most powerful drivers in our existence. Power is a good thing, but also dangerous. We will discuss mitigating and focusing these two attributes to ensure successful functioning. We will discuss as Cleckley put it, "the contrast between 'compulsive' and 'impulsive' symptoms." We are in many ways highly compulsive, but the discussion of compulsion will come in the next chapter this is the chapter on impulse.

Our impulsive behavior has the potential to be one of our strongest attributes. It forces us to action when we might otherwise stay stagnant. It also possesses some of the greatest dangers to us. It pushes us to jump even into the darkest of pits. We must limit that damage while still embracing the ability it gives us in achieving success. As the Taoists understood there is a whimsical quality to our existence. Our impulsive behavior allows us to truly embrace the whimsical aspect of the world.

Sociopaths often burn bright, burn fast, and burn out. And yet we have long term lives because like the phoenix we restart. We do not fear destruction because we know that we can easily rise again from the ashes of our current lives and burn stronger than we ever had before. We live this constant cycle of creation and destruction. Cleckley speaks of a childhood sociopath that would on a whim steal candy and then give that candy away to other children. The child was not attempting to ingratiate herself with other children, nor did she care if the other kids wanted candy. She merely felt a drive to steal, and then a drive to give it away. She lived through whimsy. In her strength, she could just give away that which she had conquered.

There are negatives to being so impulsive. Sociopaths often have no real-life plan to follow in any long-term sense. We come across to others as unreliable and lacking in many behavior controls. Because we often ignore our own rational assessment of the situation we appear to fail in learning from our experience or come across as irrational. We burn away what appear as vital parts of ourselves. That burning can hurt ourselves and others. We are potentially highly destructive forces in our world. And our drive to action can impulsively lead to great harm.

Our drive to action has positives. When other people hide

their true desires and intentions a sociopath must often act on them. We do not always have the luxury to hide away those things we want. We are forced to act, and so we have a powerful immediate driver to take the next step. It's a driver that often breaches our illusions of control and ensures that action is taken. We have an inherent understanding of the world not as consequence but as experiences. We sprint through the shadowy forest of life while the rest of the world tiptoes.

The impulsive drive to act often causes the sociopaths to embrace whimsy. Cleckley described one sociopath that decided on a whim to leave his good job and go on a trip. Upon that same whim, he proceeded in *"throwing away the keys to his car on the way in a gesture of careless bravado. At the station he stood before a timetable, closed his eyes, and put down his finger at random. Noting that he had by chance fallen on Tulsa, he bought a ticket and, bringing along a good supply of whiskey, left without more ado for that city."* When asked how leaving a good job and moving to some random new city was a good idea the patient said, "I just sold myself somehow on the idea of doing it," After several stories such as this Cleckley determined that the "sort of repugnance or other inhibiting force that would prevent any or all such impulses from being followed (or perhaps from even becoming conscious impulses) in another person is not a factor that can be counted on to play much part in the psychopath's decisions." Spiders are free, in his view, of those self-restraints that hold back flies. Instead we live in a world of whimsy and freedom.

The philosophy of Taoism is the art of studying the indefinable and following its path. It is not about having a certain faith or even a specific set of thoughts, instead it is about having a certain style of being. It is not about living with a certain set of rules or labels, but instead embracing your own heart. Most Taoist thinkers like to quote Lao Tzu. I instead prefer the whimsy and joy of Chuang Tzu. Chuang Tzu is perhaps the greatest poet and prose writer of his time, somewhere in the Chou Dynastic period. He was a contemporary of Mencius, and dealt with several Confucians and Legalists all of whom he mocked in his own humorous way. When reading the long boring philosophies of China, Chuang Tzu is a breath of fresh air. He (as Cleckley would say about most sociopaths), "appears to take a positive and boastful delight in showing off in the midst of their uninviting, destructive, and antisocial achievements." He took glee in taking down a peg those he saw as too serious. Chuang Tzu was a hero of whimsy. As Camus embraced absurdity, Chuang Tzu embraced whimsy.

There was once the question posed by an ancient king that asked three wise men the best way to cross a river. The first man (representative of Confucius) said one must plan every aspect of the river. One must study the current and the rocks. Only once the entirety of the system is understood can a person begin to safely cross. One, at that point, understands every step, they do not even need to act, or see, they just can. They just move through the motions they preplanned. The second man (representative of Lao Tzu) said it was impossible to understand the river as it will be but only as it is. So, it is better to take one step at a time. One must step forward, breath, look around and feel the moment. Each step is its own step. Each moment its own moment. After one action and before the next, a person must try to understand. The feel of the water rushing past ankles, the round hardness of the rocks under foot. Breath in that moment, and one can safely take another step. In this way, you can safely cross the river. The third man (representative of Chuang Tzu) said it is best to just dive right in and hope the rocks do not kill you before the current pulls you across.

Chuang Tzu taught that living this momentary existence allows us to understand the world as it truly is. He claimed there are in this world all kinds of masters. By master Chuang Tzu did not mean ruler, he meant master in the sense of a practitioner with great skill. He was unique in his time that he considered masters as coming in all forms, even in the most menial tasks. He spoke of maximizing any great skill through repetition, mindful attention, and accepting moment to moment.

One great master he spoke of was the Butcher of Ting who spoke of cutting up an ox. He taught the Lord Wen-hui that a good butcher sharpened their knives every month. A great butcher sharpened their knives every year. This was because the good butcher used their knife on the ox. They hacked at it. They hacked into the ox. The great butcher though saw the ox as parts, and so they cut. They cut in the space between the parts. They saw bones meet muscles and so they cut between those parts. Ting said this was skill, this learning to cut between the parts.

Ting though claimed to have gone beyond skill. He had the same knife for 19 years and had never needed to sharpen it. He did this, he claimed, because he did not see an ox, he did not see its parts. He saw the moment. By embracing that moment, breathing it in, the knife, which had no edge, fit into the spaces between the particles. In his words, "I go out to meet it with my whole spirit and don't think only about what meets the eye. Sensing and knowing. The spirit goes where it will, following the natural contours, revealing large cavities, leading the blade through openings, moving onward according to actual form." He lived that moment and within it he was a master. By training past mere skill, he could safely embrace his impulses. He could allow them to guide him through those exact moments and tasks free of the handicaps of other people and see things as the experiences they truly were. And he could delight in those experiences.

The sense of whimsy and need for delight was best outlined in a story about Chuang Tzu himself. The tale is that two great minsters came to him and offered him a position at court to advise a great ruler. He would have the best robes and most beautiful rooms. He replied by asking them if they had a "sacred turtle" at court and they said yes. He asked if it is still the practice to take a turtle and paint its shell and put it in a gilded box. Why yes, it is, they paint the shell in gold and encrust it in gems. Is the gilded box beautiful and expensive, he asked. The most beautiful of boxes ever made in all the land they replied. Chuang Tzu asked would the turtle rather be that unmoving turtle in a pretty box, or one in the wild with its tail dragging in the mud? A Sociopath like that turtle does not need to keep the trappings of societal riches, when they can be free. A sociopath is driven to act. They can never be happy cooped forever in structure, they require the excitement of freedom. They need to drag their tails in the mud.

Sociopaths are driven to act for that excitement. We have as Sorensen claims a "constant need to live on the edge." There is this drive in us when we see a thing we want to experience. We see a cliff, and we want to experience the free fall, and so we jump. We live in the pure moment. Where the flies must give in to impulse the spiders are driven by it. We are natural first adopters. This impulse, when we strive to understand it, helps us to break the illusion of control that all humans have.

There is this illusion of control people all have over their lives. They have a job and house. If they act in a certain way they can reap certain benefits. Those benefits are theirs and they can control how and when they achieve them. These are lies they tell themselves. There is no plan that will always work, no property you will always have. There is nothing in this world that you can hold or grasp onto that will not one day change or disappear. In this the Buddha was correct. All that control is an illusion. We work so hard to mimic and manipulate things as we want them, but the best laid goals sometimes fail to come to fruition. Our need to act can at times destroy our plans and burn them to the ground.

It is a good reminder, that we are stronger then we think. In many pacific northwest tribal cultures, there is the idea of a potlatch. A person planning to put on a potlatch shows their strength in two steps. First, they show their power. Through good hunting or other skillful actions, they amass wealth much as a person would in any other capitalist society. They strive to become the strongest and have the wealth to prove it. Second, they show their true strength. They give it all away. They prove they have no need for any of it, because they can overcome. They are strong, in a way that sociopaths live every day. In a way that recognizes the lack of control we all have in life. The freedom that comes not from having what you desire; but from having the power to fulfill your desires. The freedom to not be owned by them.

The illusion of control and ownership they have in their minds holds them back. It is a great weakness of the flies. Too many sociopaths never learn the lessons taught by our impulsive drive. That we have no real control over anything. We must prepare ourselves and strengthen our minds and bodies. We know there will be consequences of our actions, that to remain functioning we must prepare for. But the one honest truth about us is that we do not see the world as a path of potential consequences but as a path of experiences. The flies fear what will be with their simple slave morality, but fearing what will be keeps you from the greatest joys. As M.E. Thomas says about precautions, "precautions are expensive, either in terms of actual costs for safety or opportunity costs for risks that you could have taken but didn't." The flies miss so many experiences they could have had out of fear. The spiders though understand there is no cause and effect, only enjoyment of the now.

That is not to say sociopaths do not understand that there

are consequences. We do. There is a difference from knowing a thing and letting that thing own you. All the experts talk about how little it takes a sociopath to decide to do something. This is not because it takes so much less to drive us then it does others, it is because we do not fear the consequences of those actions. We know they are there. We know what they are likely to be. Being smarter than flies we probably know them better than they do. But the experience is what is important. We take the damage that comes not because it does not hurt us, but because the experience was more important. We accept the eventual suffering as the potential price of our joy, even when the price appears outweighed by our gain.

The world is not meant to be tiptoed through, it is meant to be enjoyed and embraced. Our drive to act is one of our greatest strengths because it forces us to truly live that amazing truth about life. We are shaped by this drive and it constantly breaks us free from the frames we would otherwise lock ourselves into. We need this freedom to truly embrace life, and if there is one great lesson we can teach the flies, it would be this, embrace every experience. Containing our drive when needed though is a lesson we must all learn to remain functioning. Though different these skills will be the same and/or similar to many of those I cover in our unique focus, and so I will wait until that section to cover the way to help focus this attribute.

Sociopaths have a need to act, this gives us the appearance of being whimsical and care free where other people are not. It means we act in high risk actions while the flies are often much more risk adverse. We embody the ideas of philosophers such as Chuang Tzu that wanted us to embrace the moment and live free of reliance on worldly goods for our happiness. This drive to act fulfills our need for excitement while breaking the illusion of control most people have. Giving us a constant lesson that we have no real control, which frees us from trying to grasp that control. We have this drive because we understand the world not as consequences but as experiences. We want to amass the experiences we can rather than the possessions others might. We are driven to act, controlling that drive is important, but knowing when to give in is equally so.

Chapter Ten:

Uniquely Focused

Sociopaths must balance our obsessive natures to become functioning. This nature allows us to be compulsively focused on tasks through their completion (or until the obsession lets go). Of course, it also sometimes forces us to fixate on a specific thing; at times to our detriment. It is a struggle because once we become focused on the object of our obsession it becomes extremely difficult to move on. This can be a huge benefit when the task at hand requires completion. We will work unstopping and unwavering until we either complete the task or the obsession wears off. I have seen sociopaths spend hours untying a knot that caught their attention. We are in the words of M.E. Thomas "proverbial pit bulls" in the centering in on our targets. Once our teeth are on the rope we hold on past all intelligence. As I went over in other sections, like "Mimicking," our unique ability to remain focused on a specific idea will act like an addiction that can be extremely beneficial to our goals. When out of control though we take on fantastic behavior to reach the specific obsession we have. We are, once in the grip of it, without many behavior controls beyond the need to reach our destination. But we can head off the obsession, focus it, and that focus will become a focus unique to spiders.

Obsessions come from what we are dealing with. From daily interests that catch our attention. First, you must begin practicing letting go of obsessions you have. This will not be easy, and when they take hold, they take hold hard. But you can do it by concentrating on the art of letting go. Second, start to focus on needs and wants. If your specific goals become your obsession, then you will more readily achieve them. You will be driven to achieve goals in ways few others will ever be able to. For daily practice the best ways to learn to focus is through physical activity. Burn it out with exercise. Competitive and goal orientated activities will supply the necessary incentives through the desire to be dominate. They will further exercise the body and mind while practice toward achieving goals. Physical exertion is highly important in keeping our mind and body focused.

The history of philosophy, especially in the western world, has been beset with the two opposing ideas of reason and passion. From all over the world and all over time the tension between these two sides of humanity are discussed. Plato described humans as having a soul being pulled by two horses, one reason and one passion. The sociopath is often believed to be pulled only by reason, but this is not true. Through our obsessive behavior (and impulsive behavior) we can be pulled hard into the direction of passion. It is the story of the old native who teaches his son that within each person live two wolves. One wolf is thoughtful and helpful while the other wolf is destructive. The wolves are in constant battle, fighting tooth and nail to overtake the body of the person. The one that wins, well that is one that the person feeds most. This idea of passions driving one direction and reason driving the other is a constant in the flies ideal. They have many-many ways of trying to control if reason or passion is the main driving force. As a sociopath, I look at this debate differently. I do not look for ways to control my passions with my reason, so much as I look to choose what is there and then focus my obsessions. As the flies, must learn to let go of unwanted passions so to must I learn to let go of unwanted obsessions.

The first step in learning to focus your obsessions is letting them go. There is an art to letting things go. An art sociopaths do not often have to practice. Sociopaths have no connection to things and so they do not have a lot to let go of. They have no anger, hate, or love. Material possessions have no real hold or value. What we do have is our obsession. It is our addiction. The final step in being free and learning to focus this attribute is to be able to let go of specific obsessions at will. This is not easy. It is a struggle to have one more chapter to read, and yet you still put the book down. I imagine a fly giving up their bank account for no other reason but proving they can. That is the level you need to reach, the thing you need to practice.

Start with simple forms of meditation. There are a multitude of mental exercises in the world and you will find your own. As stated I like simple breath exercises mixed with mantras reinforced with stare at the wall style mediation when I am in a time of peace. When I am in a state of peace and meditation I do something simple like tap my index finger with my thumb. As I do this I breath in the peace, and let it back out. I also chant my mantras quietly in my mind. You need to close your eyes and create mantras, easy phrases that represent your peace as well as simple short phrases. I use several, a few of my favorites are "I am the wind, and the wind passes through me." And, "I am everything, I am nothing." The Doctrine of Experience has several that are easy to use.

When I find myself in a moment of obsessive behavior that I feel wrongly about I pause, touch my index finger to my thumb and chant the mantra of my choice. As I do this I imagine the obsessive need bleeding away. I imagine seeing the situation from a state of peace. It does not often work, but it works enough. I find it calms me and in that moment of calm I can find my foot hold on reinstituting my focus on the tasks I prefer to set as goals. The real trick here though is not to necessarily refocus the obsession. The trick is to let it go, let it bleed away. You face the obsession, and accept it. You do not fight it, or attempt to force it away. You face it, accept it, and let it go. Like recognizing the chittering monkey in your head, you just let it go.

This can be especially difficult when dealing with disliking someone. The need to smash or ruin them. They do something that requires a painful response and that response is not always beneficial to your bottom line. A boss that is just begging to be hit, or a police officer is just acting like a complete prick. You start to become obsessed with crossing that line. But the line is not one you wish to cross. You need to let it go. You need to follow your practice, use your mantra, begin to take back your focus.

The second area of practice will be to focus the obsession rather than let it go. This is easiest done when no other obsession has currently taken root. You find goals, you have wants and needs that effect those goals. You may not be able to focus your obsession on the overarching goal, but you can focus it on small important steps. You want to be a great pianist; start by learning a song, start to read about the song you want to learn, study it practice it. I cannot tell you how many times I started to read an article on Wikipedia that I wanted to be interested in and found myself a day later still reading connected articles. Allow for a song, composer, or genre to become an obsession of the day. It will drive you to learn more and practice harder. You will need perfection, you will perfect the song. It is this ability to obsess that leads many sociopaths to greatness. You can harness it, then you can reach that greatness. You fail to harness it and it will control you.

A great method to begin harnessing your focus is to embrace physical activities, sports, and games in which you will be driven to compete. Obsession leaves a certain amount of physical tension in your body both in their completion and in their failure. To relieve this tension, you should begin a regular exercise routine in which you work yourself into exhaustion. At least part of this routine should focus on competitive sports. These sports will work your body and mind while fulling your need to dominate specific groups and tasks. You will practice focusing your obsession upon specific aspects of the sport. A good example is making three throws or a great back handed serve. You practice, over and over until you can succeed at your task. Then you move on, all geared toward perfecting the sport. Push yourself as only you can. Accompany the physical activity with mental games. These games should push you to think hard and make you concentrate to win. But do not become obsessed with winning, become obsessed with specific aspects and skill needs of the games. Do not allow the obvious goals to become the obsessions.

Choose your obsessions, focus them, focus where to find them, practice them.

The sociopathic obsessive compulsion is a strong driver of behavior for us. It is a strong benefit in ensuring we focus on specific tasks we need accomplished. This strength can though become a detriment when it is not handled correctly. A good spider must learn to live with the obsessions and how to shape them. Like harnessing electricity one must learn to channel it, but first one must learn to turn it on and off as needed. You learn to turn it off through practicing letting go. Using mediation and other mental focus based techniques you can learn to let go once an obsession takes hold. Use these techniques to limit the damaging aspects of a harmful obsession. Once you have learned to let go, you will then wish to begin learning to focus your obsessive qualities. This focus is great for accomplishing complex tasks that require hard work and dedication. Learning this focus through picking small sections of a task rather than an overarching goal. You are more likely to hold the obsession if the task is short term. You can begin daily practice by embracing physical activities that are strenuous and contain some competitive elements. Playing sports and games that will both strengthen the body and focus the mind will only work to ensure you become a better sociopath.

Obsession is like all the other attributes found in this section. They are strengths built into us because we are better than the flies. But those strengths, every one of them, have the potential to become weaknesses. If we as sociopaths allow our attributes to control us or they are not practiced to ensure artistry, then these amazing parts of us will become detriments. The attributes of impulse and obsession are the pinnacle of this. They have the potential to raise us up and the power to crash us back down. I cannot stress enough the need to self-evaluate in these areas to ensure you will be able to truly intertwine all of our attributes.

We have gone over each attribute here and embraced how to first understand and then improve each one. The functioning sociopaths have the potential to become the greatest artists of the world. They can blend together the colors of their own being and the beings around them to ensure beautiful creations are made that will be moments of awe inspiring experience. We are artists of experience that will continue to change the world.

Section 3.

The Doctrine of Experience

Ramblings of a Sociopath

From Hume, we learned that what we know about the world is gathered through our perceptions of it. Barring any belief that we have some innate knowledge built in, we are born knowing nothing. As we grow we fill that emptiness with experiences through perception. We base all knowledge off our historical experiences. Learning in all its forms is dependent upon this ability to experience. In the attempt to know more we must learn, to learn we must experience. To grow as living things, we must experience more. Experience at that point becomes our goal. Whether you are experiencing a book you are reading, a class you are taking, or jumping out of an airplane you build from the experiences you are having. You combine those experiences in your mind through memories and contemplations.

It is not enough to do a thing. In a meaningless existence if one chooses to act they must act well. When there are no reasons to act, action must be its own reason. The apathy of the world gives rise to a desire to do those things one does well. To be the best at a thing is a great feeling. And feelings are just one more experience to learn from. This idea springs from artistic impulses. There is no reason to create art, and yet humans do. To overcome apathy and begin a work of art then is a striving for perfection. The meaning of perfection here is a personal perfection. Without meaning and purpose in the world there is no measurement of which to judge inherent perfection. The perfection then in this and all instances is a subjective ideal. This is even more reason to reach for the standard.

To decide to act one must become an artist in what they do. Like Chuang Tzu before us we must search to become masters in even the smallest actions. As masters, we are artists. The creation of our lives is a work of art, and every action is a brush stroke. We must embrace those strokes while still putting thought into each one. The level of skill that must be achieved to truly take up this task is monumental. We are enough though, each of us. We stand in a land of chaos and whimsy. Because of the lack of order, we are inherently free. We are free from purpose beyond which we attribute to ourselves. From the depths of what we are we are free. Free to seek after our experiences.

We must become artists of those experiences. Take charge of them and shape them. We have such a limited time upon this world we must fill it with new and beautiful things. Fill up our insides with perceptions to grow us. There is so little to what we are, it is paramount that we grow it. When we die, there is a moment. That moment is our lives. It does not matter what we leave behind, only what we take with us. Our lives must be al dente, they must be firm to the tooth. We must become chefs and create dish so flavorful the world weeps at our passing.

We are not our indoctrination. Society wants to create a boring old nothing that obeys and fits. But we are artists. We create beauty. That beauty shapes and frames every moment of what we are. We must let go of the rules and systems that make up what is and create our own. What do we have though if the past we have perceived is an untrustworthy guide. We have feelings. If there is any innate knowledge built within us absent perception, then feelings are that innate knowledge. Desire is the built-in instinct that helps to guide us past our indoctrinations. It is the light that leads us from the darkness. It informs us what we seek in our experiences. It informs our art. It informs the overall painting while our skill guides our brush strokes. These two things must work together then, our skill and our instinct. They create our art and so shape our lives.

Have you ever painted a picture? Have you sat down and looked at blank canvas with pencil and brushes? You look at each paint you have. You think of ideas on how to mix them. You are restricted by the palate and tools you have. But your skill can take even the smallest supply and mix a great work. You are free to use the tools you have as you wish, but you are restricted by the tools at hand. Still you create the work. You sketch it out and apply the paints. You rework the paints over and over. You fix the colors, and adjust the tone. You constantly repaint and reshape what is until you reach perfection. But all artists know that there is never a completion, never a perfection. You must keep at it until you finally give up, and move on to a new work. An artist knows even old works they look upon have touches that they need to fix. Artists are their own worst critiques. The need to constantly build and edit is forever.

We know what we are. We know the attributes that make us. We know how to shape them and use them to the benefit of our world and our art. But what behaviors make us great? What doctrine can take root and grow into a thing of beauty? How do we ensure that we take up the mantle of both artist and art? We do this through the Doctrine of Experience.

The Doctrine of Experience

1. I am an artist of experience.
2. I am my own work of art.
3. I am the wind and all that is passes through me.
4. I am nobody and nothing.
5. I am the leaf upon the wind.
6. I am the libertine.
7. I am the now.
8. I am the objective observer.
9. I am my own master.
10. I am beholden only to power.

"I am an artist of experience." One will live experiences, one will not put them off latter then they must. One will live them regardless of potential fears. One must shape the experience of themselves and others.

Systems of commandments are built on overarching ideas and this entire list is based on this one idea. The human existence is constructed on a search for experiences. This search is the overarching goal of all life. There is no inherent meaning in the world, there is only the moment to moment experiences that build our lives. The creation then of those experiences is paramount to a life well lived.

"I am my own work of art." One will do all things with panache and style. It is not enough to be a thing one must be the best and most beautiful version of that thing. Good enough is not enough, one must be perfection. One controls how one is seen. One is never a being but always becoming. One's life is a constant edit of what was.

To maximize experience a person must treat their own life as a work of art. They must be the artist and the creation. They must create beautiful things through a mixture of design and instinct. Like a good jazz song or a well-made sculpture the person will create themselves. The work will never be completed. There will never be a state of being, it will never be complete. A constant state of becoming will work to ensure the work is in a constant state of seeking after perfection. One must put thought and effort in every moment as they work to create that which they are. They will work to shape not only their own experiences but the experience of others. They will become a thing of beauty for the world to share.

"I am the wind and all that is passes through me." There is nothing in this world one cannot let go of. One is not their possessions. They are not even themselves, they are the wind.

This is a personal refusal to hold onto anything. Like a

sculptor that cuts the excess away from the stone one must be willing to cut away anything that endangers the experience. A possession may help the enjoyment of an experience but once the experience is over it may become a detriment. A weight holding one down. Like the Buddhist that leaves the raft upon the river bank so too must one be willing to leave everything behind. One has no self beyond the experiences they are partaking. One grasps onto nothing, they must let it all go. They live their world unattached to everything but the experience.

"I am nobody and nothing." One will not lie to themselves that they are special. Greatness takes work. One will do that work. One is not their persona and it is not them. One is unseen by the world and they embrace that. To be hidden is to be free.

This is a personal refusal to allow the self to be held onto. The world is nothing but a set conglomeration of experiences. There is no underlying world or inherent meaning within that world. This includes all humans. It is a desire by many to feel special or real. But this is a lie to comfort one and hide the beautiful truth. One is only the current experience they have, and their only legacy is the experience they give to others. There is only the perception of reality. One must accept that they are nothing, that deep down they are nobody. The universe is a huge meaningless accumulation of matter. This frees one from the attachments that keep them from fulfilling their potential experiences. It is a removal of shackles that held one back.

"I am the leaf upon the wind." One embraces freedom in all its forms. Nothing can chain them. Nothing can grasp them. One passes through life untouched by everything around them.

This is a personal refusal to allow the world to grasp and hold. It is not enough to be nothing; the world is also nothing. There is nothing to grasp or be grasped by. The world will attempt to solidify what a person is and hold them into that box. This will limit the ability to have experiences and the experiences that one might have. Freedom must be kept dear and fought for so that nothing is held back. The grasping hands of the world must be slipped and the chains broken. Experiences must be sought, and only with freedom will the full gamut of possibilities be possible. One must ensure all aspects of their being are free to fully find the experiences they can have.

"I am the libertine." One will embrace their desires. Ones very being is a conglomeration of desires and one will feel shame for none of them as they fulfill them all.

Shame for what one desires is a hindrance to experience. The desires of the body and mind are natural drivers to guide one. Because there is nothing but perception and experience the guiding light through the darkness is desire. Listening to that voice without judgement or blocks is the only way to find the experiences that will best fulfill one's life. Shame reflects social indoctrination and only by removing all indoctrinations will one be free. The chains of society must be broken.

"I am the now." One is not the past. One is untouched by regret. One has no understanding of guilt or shame. The past is unchangeable and gone, it is no business of the one.

The past is a chain upon one's neck. It must be broken. There is no guilt or shame for that which has past, there is only freedom. By living now and only now one is free from those constraints that hold back enjoyment of the current experiences. One must be free to enjoy a work of art for itself. Attempting to allow other works to bleed into it take away from the experience the artist intended. The artist is the one. To truly enjoy the full range of that one experience, the past must be let go of.

"I am the objective observer." One has no bias except their reasoning skills. One is the skeptical stoic. One does not allow emotions or preconceived ideas to see the world for them. There is no emotional panic within one. The one only observes the world using reason. The one does not judge, only experiences.

Emotions get in the way of perceiving the now. Reason allows one to see things for what they are. An objective observer sees the world around them for what it is; uncolored by preconceived ideas. Emotions create moments of emotional panic when one needs to let go of things that appear vital. Evaluating the world through murky lenses creates an inability to truly experience the moment in all its glory. It creates a blinder and a chain that shadows and highlights the new and abnormal. The world must be experienced as is for a complete experience of the moment. It is a source of power to see what is.

"I am my own master." One is the alpha of their pack. It is natural for one to seek dominance, so seek it over oneself. One may not be the leader but they are still responsible to fulfill their own potential. Power is the only guide, and it is the one's responsibility to ensure it is maximized.

Power is paramount to fulfill one's desires and obtain one's experiences. Seeking to better oneself is natural. Going to school to get an education gives one a chance to learn important skills and get a degree. These things will help one to make more money, which will allow one to afford to have the experiences they desire. Only the top members of the pack have an unlimited range of experiences possible. Reaching that point of the hierarchy ensures one has the options desired to fulfill those experiences. Regardless of where one finds themselves on the hierarchy, they must still be their own master.

The mind and actions of a person are under their own control. One rules and is ruled by themselves only, and only by themselves. To exert true dominance is to exert it over oneself only. It is the goal to be free of enslavement not to enslave the free. Understanding that all people are free to choose their own path means that their path is not for others to choose. True dominance is possible only within oneself. One must embrace that fact and exert their power where they can, internally.

"I am beholden only to power." One should only submit to those stronger than they are, and only so long as the strength persists. Power is the currency of nature. Whether it is money, knowledge, or any other form of power it is how one obtains one's goals.

The student bows to the power of the teacher's knowledge. The student remains under the teacher until they have learned the knowledge for themselves. At which point the teacher no longer has power the student requires and so the student moves on. The submission of the student is a natural state. Joining to those with power gives one a level of freedom that opposing them does not.

It is natural for the teacher to teach. The true proof of power is to be able to give it away and still exert it. To give power is to take it as well. The power to feed the masses and teach the downtrodden is one of the greatest powers in the world. To shape their experience is an experience in and of itself.

About the Author

Alcibiades Anon is the pseudonym for a highly functioning sociopath that likes to hear herself speak even while remaining silent. As a philosopher, Anon has spent a lifetime exerting his influence over the world and now, as she gets older, he had a whim to teach her thoughts to the young sociopaths around him. The ongoing knowledge and tools she wishes to impart are his last great gift to humankind. Anon often rambles and dreams and loves a good tangent but the quality of his lessons are apparent for those that can see them. Anon dreams of a world where she and those like him do not need to hide what they are, while believing even in that world she would likely remain hidden.

If you have enjoyed the book please feel free to check out the author's blog at:

https://sociopathphilosophy.wordpress.com

Description of the Book.

The Trickster's Path is one sociopath's attempt to understand himself and others like her. The Trickster's Path uses the theories of experts and other sociopaths to describe what exactly a sociopath is. The Trickster's Path goes further to break the different areas of sociopathic tendencies into attributes. Anon uses those attributes to describe how he has remained functioning in the world she finds so alien. The book rambles and takes multiple tangents as Anon self discovers what he and those like her are. The Trickster's Path is an honest portrayal of one person's attempt to understand himself and deal with the world around her.

www.ingramcontent.com/pod-product-compliance
Lightning Source LLC
Chambersburg PA
CBHW062159280526
45788CB00001B/371

* 9 7 8 1 5 4 2 8 3 6 7 9 1 *